D1372436

# ARTHUR MILLER

GENIUS!
The Artist and the Process

# ARTHUR MILLER

by

Bruce Glassman

## GENIUS!
### The Artist and the Process

SILVER BURDETT PRESS

**Created and produced by:** Blackbirch Graphics, Inc.

**Project Editor:** Emily Easton
**Designer:** Cynthia Minichino
**Cover Design:** Leslie Bauman

Manufactured in The United States of America

10   9   8   7   6   5   4   3   2   1

**Library of Congress Cataloging-in-Publication Data**
Glassman, Bruce.
   Arthur Miller / by Bruce Glassman.
   (Genius!)
   Includes bibliographical references.
   Summary: Discusses the life of the major American playwright and examines the common themes explored in his works.
   1. Miller, Arthur, 1915–  —Juvenile literature.  2. Dramatists, American—20th century—Biography—Juvenile literature.
[1. Miller, Arthur, 1915–  .  2. Dramatists, American.]  I. Title.
II. Series: Genius! (Englewood Cliffs, N.J.) PS3525.I5156Z65   1990
812′.52—dc20 [B] [92] 80-30498
ISBN 0-382-09904-4 (lib. bdg.)                   CIP
ISBN 0-382-24032-4                                AC

(*Frontispiece*)
For more than fifty years, Arthur Miller has explored the American heart and mind and has revealed us to ourselves as few artists have.

# Contents

*A man sits down at a typewriter with some blank paper on which he types image-describing words, and at a certain point turns around and confronts some four or five hundred people, and trucks and food wagons, airplanes, horses, hotels, roads, cars, lights, all of which he has by some means, untraceable now in its complexity, evoked from nowhere and nothing. Oddly, he ends up with little power over these results of his imagination; they go their own way with not the slightest awareness that they owe their current incarnation to him.*
—Arthur Miller
On the filming of *The Misfits*

Miller (*left*) and his older brother, Kermit. The boys grew up in
Harlem, then a fashionable neighborhood.

# CHAPTER 1

# HARLEM DAYS

*An ambiguous place, Harlem was packed nevertheless*
*with the living and much hope.*
—Arthur Miller, on his childhood neighborhood

There is a popular misconception throughout the world that writers have to suffer in order to be great. While it is true that many of the world's artists have battled alcoholism, drugs, failed marriages, broken homes, and ridicule, not all creative figures spring from such struggles. Arthur Miller's early years were, for example, rather unremarkable.

Born into a happy and secure Jewish family on 112th Street, October 17, 1915, most of young Arthur's struggles stemmed from his emulation of his older brother Kermit, who set a hard example to live up to. Kermit was always the "good looking" brother, the athletic and outgoing one who was popular in school and for whom their father had the greatest hopes. Arthur, in contrast, was not a terribly good-looking or popular young man. Though he spent much of his early adolescence playing football and other school sports, he soon felt like an outcast. Young Arthur's interests more often lay in books and discussions about the world. Kermit, who as an adult became a salesman, surely influenced his brother's writing and, most probably, was the primary model for Biff Loman, the oldest son in *Death of a Salesman*.

Arthur's parents, Augusta and Isadore, had both grown up in hard-working immigrant families that were driven to succeed in America at any cost.

His mother, Augusta, had been born on Broome Street on the lower east side of New York City, the daughter of a Polish immigrant from Radomizl named Louis Barnett. Mr. Barnett ran a fairly successful clothing business in Manhattan and was busily expanding this enterprise when his daughter was born.

Miller's father, Isadore, was born in Radomizl, Poland, and had been left there with family friends at the age of six by his parents when they sailed to America in order to find a better life for themselves. A few months later they wired the young boy a ticket and had him sent to New York to join them. When Isadore finally arrived, after three weeks in steerage, his teeth were loose and he had scabs on his head. His ten-year-old-brother Abe picked him up at Castle Garden and brought him to the family on Stanton Street. His father, Samuel Miller, was now in the clothing business and too busy at his factory to pick up his son.

As a father, Isadore Miller continued the family tradition of providing for his wife and children through hard work, faith in the opportunity of America, and by maintaining a strong moral character. As a religious Jew, Isadore taught his children about the importance

Arthur's mother, Augusta Miller, promoted a rich intellectual life and love of literature. Isadore, Arthur's father, tried to instill in his sons an ethical sense of behavior and political responsibility.

of ethical behavior and the duty of all people to become politically involved in the world. This tradition had a lasting effect on Arthur, on how he thought about writing and how he saw men—such as his father—who worked all their lives to "become something" while they tried to keep a grasp on the traditions and virtues they felt were most important. His father's (and his grandfather's) emotional convictions and blunt ways of expressing their ideals would provide a basis for many father characters in plays to come, including *No Villain, The Price,* and *Death of a Salesman.*

The Jewish immigrant community in which Arthur grew up was small and most of its members shared the dream of succeeding in America. Many of these immigrants had come to the United States before World War I broke out in Europe in 1914. Others had

At the turn of the century, immigrants poured into Ellis Island in search of a better life in America.

the good fortune to escape during the conflict. Once in the United States, these energetic and hopeful people felt a sense of relief and safety at being in a free country. The overall feeling on the streets, and the message that was conveyed to the neighborhood's children, was that anything could happen if one worked hard enough and was in the right place at the right time. At the time of Arthur Miller's birth, a well-known but unscrupulous man in New York clothing circles, Bill Fox, came to a few of his associates for some money to help him finance a film studio in California. One of the people he asked for backing was Isadore Miller who, knowing of Fox's reputation as a cheat, turned him down. A few years later Fox would build his studio—known today as Twentieth Century-Fox. New York was full of opportunities in 1915.

The atmosphere of lively discussion and political debate that was constantly a part of the Miller household sunk into young Arthur's consciousness. This rich verbal tradition, one of storytelling and of trading intellectual ideas, would help to form the unique talent that was soon to emerge in Arthur Miller.

In 1921 (the year in which his younger sister Joan was born), at the age of six, young Arthur started school. While much of the rest of the world was still recovering from the enormous devastation of the war, America was enjoying an economic boom. The general outlook of the country was sunny, glad to be at peace and ready to build an exciting and prosperous future. Arthur, still innocent and somewhat sheltered by the Jewish community, had never heard of, or experienced, anti-Semitism.

It was at this time that Arthur saw his first movie, an event he recalls as a "haunting experience." It took place on a rooftop in Harlem, and the film was projected on a bedsheet instead of a screen. The images

Morningside Avenue in Harlem, around the time of Arthur Miller's birth.

and the experience of that night stayed with him forever. Later, when his mother took him to the Shubert Theater to see his first stage play (Augusta was a regular theatergoer), Arthur realized the difference between films and stage plays. At the age of eight he perceived that they represented "two kinds of reality." He decided then that "the stage was far more real."

As a young Jew in a religious household, Arthur was taught very early to respect books and the ideas they conveyed. (He would frequently be scolded by Kermit for leaving a book open on its spine.) He first realized that writers were real people when he came across a full-page illustration of Charles Dickens set against a background of some of his characters in *The Book of Knowledge*. This portrait of Dickens fascinated the young boy, who was an avid fan of *Oliver Twist*.

His teenage years were uneventful, plagued with the usual awkwardness of teenage sexuality and a new awareness of the opposite sex. Miller, at this time, tried to be more an athlete than an academic, and he and his brother were quite similar to the young Biff and Happy of *Death of a Salesman*. The most significant event during Arthur's years at James Madison High School was the stock market crash of October 1929 and the subsequent onset of the Great Depression. As a young and impressionable high school student in 1929, he felt terribly frightened by the sudden change in the country's mood. It all happened so fast and took such a serious toll on the quality of life in America. Suddenly people were broke, out of work, without hope, and without any dreams of a bright future.

The Depression was still in full swing when Arthur graduated from high school. After applying to the University of Michigan and being rejected for his poor academic record in high school (he failed algebra three times), Arthur had hopes of singing on the radio and becoming a star like Bing Crosby, making millions of dollars and gaining the admiration of thousands. He lined up an agent, a neighborhood wheeler-dealer named Harry Rosenthal, who peddled songs to publishers. Rosenthal, who thought Arthur had a nice tenor voice, would frequently take him to the Brill Building in Manhattan to audition for singing jobs. Rosenthal even set up a radio show for his young find, a non-paying performance at a Brooklyn radio station. He was accompanied by a blind, arthritic pianist who had emphysema and a wheeze that could be heard as plainly as Arthur's singing. The crooner was told to bill himself as a "young Al Jolson," but something about this direction made Arthur feel uneasy. Deep down, he felt as if he was being pushed in a direction in which he did not want to go. After a few more disappointing jobs and a general lack of enthusiasm for the entertainment business, the young tenor formally decided singing was not his calling.

The Depression hit his father's first business rather hard, forcing it to close after a prolonged struggle. Isadore became depressed and listless, and Kermit was forced to drop out of New York University to help his father start a new coat business, which also eventually failed. In his attempt to help the family financially, Arthur held various jobs at the coat factory. It was his difficult experiences with the arrogant, brusque buyers at the coat company that first exposed Miller to the unfair ways in which the company's salesmen were being treated. Upon leaving his father's firm, Miller wrote an unpublished short story, entitled *In Memoriam*, about the plight of a salesman. This early work was the first to explore the themes and ideas that would eventually become *Death of a Salesman*.

It was during this period, at the age of seventeen, that Arthur was first exposed to the idea of Marxism. It made a profound impression on him as a teenager and would greatly influence the rest of his life. He was outside Dozick's drugstore, where he and his friends played handball, when a college student stopped to talk. Arthur could never recall the name nor the face of the boy, but what he said would remain with him forever. The college student told Arthur that there were "really two classes of people in our society: the workers and the employers." The student went on to say that all over the world a revolution was slowly brewing that would transform everyone's life. Soon, the student continued, things would be produced for use rather than for personal profit. Then there would be more for everyone to share. Justice would reign everywhere. Miller recalls that he "understood [the student] instantly" and that he stopped playing ball to talk with him. The playwright attributes much to this spontaneous discussion on that one day. Speaking about the creation of *The Crucible*—one of his most-performed and most political works, Miller wrote in his autobiography:

> Two decades after that fateful handball game, when I was at the Salem Historical Society studying the record of the Salem witch trials of 1692, I could fairly hear the voices of those hanging judges. . . . In fact, I would probably not have been in Salem at all had I not found Marx in the middle of that handball game.

This exposure to Marxism, which so affected Miller's politics and art, was purely chance. But many of the things that would happen to Arthur Miller in the future simply happened by chance.

As a student at the University of Michigan, Miller won two Hopwood awards for excellence in playwriting.

# CHAPTER 2

# THE FIRST PLAYS

*Like most playwrights, I am part actor.*
—Arthur Miller

**A**fter Arthur's short career at his father's coat company, he began to seek other ways to support himself. At the same time, his exposure to Marxism, and his natural curiosity about ideas, motivated him to enroll in college in 1932. By 1933, after nearly a year in school, Arthur was forced to leave City College in New York due to simple exhaustion. He was trying to hold a full-time job as well as maintain a full academic schedule. Unfortunately, given the economic circumstances of the time, his schooling was the first thing to be sacrificed. But by 1934, Miller was back on the academic track, and finally was accepted and enrolled at the University of Michigan.

It was said at that time that the University of Michigan campus was filled with radical students and leftist professors. This was just a myth; the school did, however, have what Miller called "democratic attitudes" and a number of unconventional faculty members who, although they usually disagreed with its theories, openly discussed Marxism in the classroom.

*No Villain*, a play written in 1935, was Arthur Miller's first dramatic work. Using members of his family as models, he constructed a story of a garment factory strike that pitted a father against his college-educated, socialist son. Miller later described the characters as "the most autobiographical" he had ever created. Not only was the setting taken from the Miller family business, but the characters of father and son bore a striking resemblance to Isadore and Arthur.

Holding down two jobs as well as doing his schoolwork, Miller wrote *No Villain* primarily as a shot at the Hopwood Award, the University of Michigan's theater prize. In 1936 he won the award. He had hardly cashed the prize check when he was struck with a sinking feeling that he would never find another thing about which to write. It was a feeling that would come and go in him for the rest of his life.

But that worry soon disappeared. If anything, his first success inspired the young writer to write quickly and with great enthusiasm. In his autobiography, *Timebends*, Miller recalls some of his early feelings about writing:

> From the beginning, the idea of writing a play was entwined with my very conception of myself. Playwriting was an act of self-discovery from the start and would always be; it was a kind of license to say the unspeakable, and I would never write anything good that did not somehow make me blush. From the beginning, writing meant freedom. . . . It was a sort of blessing I invented for myself.

After *No Villain* came another work, entitled *Honors at Dawn*. It was the story of a prison psychiatrist who "struggles to keep the sane from moving over into madness." In this play, which also won the Hopwood Award, the central conflict is between two brothers. This work seemed to foreshadow his next serious piece, which also took place in a prison.

In Miller's senior year he wrote *The Great Disobedience*, based on firsthand research at the Jackson State Penitentiary. It was the first play he had ever researched, and it was this idea of exploring unknown worlds that showed the young writer that not every

In 1939, there was a good deal of popular support in the United States for Russia and its policies.

subject needs to spring entirely from one's personal history. "I wanted to get out of myself and use the world as my subject," he wrote. It also trained the playwright to research topics of social or political interest to him, which enabled him to construct dramas of social or political import.

*The Great Disobedience*, unlike his two previous plays, did not earn Miller a third Hopwood Award. Deemed something of a failure by the prize judges, the play was called "turgid" and inaccessible. But the experience Miller gained as a writer was much more valuable than any award could have been. In addition to exploring new worlds and the possibility of new subjects through research, *The Great Disobedience* stirred in him a new conviction that somehow his art should help to change society. This sense came partly from his realization that drama can both speak of social and human conditions and comment on them in powerful ways. The playwright speaks through his characters; he has an audience's ear, and the tricky responsibility of controlling what amounts to a one-way conversation. However appealing this power was, Miller quickly realized that it had to be held in check, for misusing it could ultimately ruin a play.

Miller graduated from the University of Michigan in 1938 and began living with his college girlfriend, Mary Grace Slattery. The two years after graduation were spent working on various plays, one of which was a grand-scale tragedy about Montezuma's destruction at the hands of Cortez. Though the play was never completed, it did provide the foundation for a later work entitled *The Man Who Had All the Luck*.

In his first two years out of school, Miller got a job with the Federal Theater Project in New York for $23 a week. He was offered a job as a writer for Twentieth Century-Fox, which paid $250 a week, but he turned it down fearing that Hollywood would destroy both his will to write about important subjects and his desire to make his work more "important" than mere entertainment. He knew of Hollywood's reputation for "using people up" and then discarding them. And the whole movie industry seemed to him a vast collection of talented people who were more concerned with money and power than with being artists.

Another aspect of Hollywood, the movie business in particular, made Miller's decision to work for the Federal Theater Project even easier. He knew he wouldn't be able to stand the process of making movies in Hollywood. The idea of having his work changed by committee, of having so many hands involved, of changing content for seemingly trivial reasons was unthinkable. Miller wrote:

> The very idea of someone editing a play of mine or so much as changing a word was enough to make my skin crawl, and to actually submit pages to a producer who became the owner of what one wrote the moment one wrote it—this was unconscionable. Indeed, the very process itself of exchanging art for money was repulsive.

It would be twenty years before Arthur Miller actually wrote a screenplay that he took to Hollywood to turn into a movie. However, in the case of *The Misfits*, he was writing not for himself, but for someone he loved very dearly.

Miller had two children while married to Mary Grace Slattery, Robert and Jane. He maintained a close relationship with both his children even after his divorce from Mary.

# CHAPTER 3

# A NEW LIFE

*In truth I would have sworn I had not changed, only the public perception of me had, but this is merely fame's first illusion.*
*—Arthur Miller*

The year 1940 was something of a turning point for Arthur Miller. Though he had already written four or five full-length plays and had gotten some encouraging interest from New York producers and actors, he began to feel as if he were "battling time." He became somewhat impatient with his writing, fearing that he would never produce any works that would make him feel "significant."

Perhaps it was his need to make visible progress, to move forward, that inspired him to marry Mary Slattery on August 5 of that year. He was twenty-five. There was some conflict involved in their marrying; she was Catholic and he Jewish and "intermarriage" in

1940 was frowned upon. In the case of Arthur and Mary, neither family was happy that their respective children had planned to make the bond official. And while religious conflict cannot be blamed for the failure of their marriage more than sixteen years later, it was nonetheless a constant source of irritation for them both.

As Mrs. Miller, Mary began work as a waitress and then as an editor at Harper & Bros. in an effort to support her new husband's pursuit of writing. A week after the wedding, the young bridegroom was already off by himself on a freighter, researching life at sea for a new play. The driving force for this project stemmed from several sources, but the primary one was his constant desire to accumulate new experiences rather than just read about them in books. As he wrote, "I wanted to rush to meet my life and my nature." But the fact that many other great American writers—Jack London and Eugene O'Neill in particular—had spent a good deal of time at sea probably didn't go unnoticed by the aspiring writer.

Just before the wedding, Miller had sold his first radio play to the Columbia Workshop, a CBS experimental series under the direction of Norman Corwin. The play, a political satire, was called *The Pussycat and the Expert Plumber Who Was a Man*. The show was broadcast while its author was at sea, and that experience gave him, for the first time, a "strange sense of power at being able to leave my voice, in effect, speaking in my absence."

Soon after that premiere, Miller began to write patriotic plays for the radio. The effort, he said, was something of a justification for his not participating in the war that America finally entered in 1941. The stories he wrote were not as deeply felt as his personal works, but as a writer during wartime (one who felt

Broadway's bright lights have always been a lure to ambitious playwrights.

guilty about being rejected from military service because of an old football injury), he felt it was his duty to boost morale with patriotic stories of bravery and the triumph of democracy. Besides, each play brought in $500, not a bad fee for a young writer in 1941. During this time, Miller also did extensive research for a screenplay he wanted to write entitled *The Story of G.I. Joe*. The screenplay never quite materialized, but his research would prove useful within a year, when he began work on another war-related project.

It was a recommendation from theatrical producer Herman Shumlin that got Arthur Miller involved in a Hollywood project in 1943. Lester Cowan, a friend of Shumlin's and a Hollywood producer, wanted a screenplay written from a collection of newspaper columns written by war reporter Ernie Pyle of United Press. Miller was offered $750 a week to take Pyle's material and write a movie to be titled *Here Is Your War*. Unfortunately, the project ran into the very problems he had always anticipated when it came to working in Hollywood: too many people wanted too much control. And the kind of control they demanded, particularly the military, went far beyond simple editing or rewriting—it involved actual control of the characters and the storyline. Unable to tolerate the process, Miller left the project. But his research did not go completely to waste; Miller turned it into a book about army training entitled *Situation Normal*.

The months since his college graduation and his subsequent marriage had been filled with profound changes, both for Miller and for the United States. Miller had given up bachelorhood and had finally started a career as a professional writer. The United States, more significantly, had given up two decades of blissful isolation from the rest of the world and had been transformed from a sleeping eagle to an angry one. And, just as America was faced with many new challenges and responsibilities during wartime, so was the young playwright. For Miller, this was a time of new thoughts and new inspirations about the nature of society and the cruelty of human fate—new thoughts that would soon be expressed in works for the stage.

Miller's next project started as a novel, entitled *The Man Who Had All the Luck*. The plot concerns the values of Middle America, but it also raises many questions about American society. Inspired in part by the story of Mary Miller's aunt Helen, whose husband had recently committed suicide, *The Man Who Had All the Luck* deals with "the question of the justice of fate" and the "irreality of success and power." The plot involves two men, seeming equals, who wind up with very different fates; one man succeeds in his life and the other fails miserably.

The play was originally written about two friends, David and Amos. David is an orphan who has rather miraculously made his way up the ladder of success in a small town. His friend Amos is a baseball player whose father, Pat, has fanatically trained his son to play baseball from the time he could walk. But it is the father's overprotectiveness that ultimately causes Amos' failure; the failure simply emphasizes David's success and underscores the cruelty of fate.

As the early drafts of *The Man Who Had All the Luck* were completed, another story element occurred to the playwright:

> One day, quite suddenly, I saw that Amos and David were brothers and Pat their father. There was a different anguish in the story now, an indescribable new certainty that I could speak from deep within myself, had seen something no one else had ever seen.

With this spontaneous realization, the young writer became better aware of his own creative process and

Harold Clurman (*left*), head of the Group Theater in New York City, was a long-time supporter of Miller's work.

learned how quickly one idea can spark another, seemingly independent of the playwright.

After months of futilely trying to find a publisher, Miller adapted *The Man Who Had All the Luck* for the stage and spent three years looking for a producer. Finally, the play was picked up and, in 1944, provided the young playwright with his Broadway debut. (That year also provided Miller with his debut as a father. His first child, Jane, was born on September 7.)

Unfortunately, *The Man Who Had All the Luck* had only "four sad performances" and then disappeared forever. Miller attributes some of the play's failure to the nature of the Broadway theater at the time. American theater, as he explained, was going through a "classical phase" that had very strict guidelines for plot and action and allowed very little variation. Audiences in the forties wanted "stories"—entertainment—and were impatient with anything that tried to make them think too hard. Miller's style, with its reliance on dialogue and its "intellectual" themes, did not quite fit that mold.

The failure of this play fulfilled a certain important function for Miller. It was through the evolution of the story, and what seemed to be the endless drafts for production, that Miller felt he began to "find himself as a playwright and perhaps even as a person." *The Man Who Had All the Luck* also proved to be a precursor to *Death of A Salesman*, Miller's masterpiece, which was written only five years later. Both plays explored the lack of justice in the failure of a "common man" as well as the intricate workings of family conflicts. And so it was through the frustrating experience of failing at his Broadway debut that Arthur Miller realized how much can be learned from failure as well as success.

The writer's realizations about the value of failure would often come to him again in the years to follow. In 1945, with the defeat of *The Man Who Had All the Luck* still fresh, Miller decided he would not write another play. He had by now already completed six or seven full-length plays since he began writing and felt that they had gotten him nowhere. As a result, he again turned his efforts to writing a novel—the only one he ever completed—entitled *Focus*. The novel, which dealt with the destructive power of anti-Semitism, was not received with great enthusiasm. It

Edward G. Robinson played Joe Keller in the film version of
*All My Sons*.

wasn't until he spoke with drama critic John Anderson (the first critic he had ever met) that he began to think once more about *The Man Who Had All the Luck*. Anderson had been intrigued by the work, and encouraged Miller to take a closer look at the play. He pointed out that a "doom hangs over the play, something that promises tragedy." These insights spurred the young playwright to look at the work again, with renewed confidence. In many ways, Miller credits the critic with saving his career as a playwright; had it not been for his conversation with Anderson, there might never have been another play from Arthur Miller. And if that is true, Miller was lucky to meet the critic when he did. For three weeks after their conversation, John Anderson died of meningitis.

At age thirty, with two or three recently written and unproduced plays, Arthur Miller took what he considered to be his last shot at playwriting. He remembers thinking at the time, "I knew playwrights nearing forty who were still awaiting their debut, but life was too interesting to waste in hanging around producer's doors." It was with this resolve that he began work on *All My Sons*, a play about a man who makes airplane parts for the military during the war and is forced to ship what he knows to be inferior parts to the army for use. The consequences of his actions turn out to be far graver than he ever anticipated; the defective parts cause the death of many soldiers, including his own son (who commits suicide). The play illustrates the tragic nature of a man who is forced to compromise his morals in order to keep both his livelihood and his respectable place in society intact. When faced with a crucial moral decision—on which the survival of his business depends—Joe Keller takes a chance and proceeds with a course of action he knows is unwise. The play points out the ultimately tragic consequences of ethical compromise, and Joe Keller, like the figures in many Greek tragedies, commits suicide to atone for his sins.

*All My Sons*, Miller vowed, would be a flawless work; each line written and rewritten until it was perfect. He had to feel that this effort was, in fact, the best one he could possibly make, since the fate of his writing career was at stake. If he failed, at least he would fail with something he firmly believed was quality work.

After two years of painstaking rewrites, *All My Sons* was complete and in the mail to Herman Shumlin, the producer and director of all of Lillian Hellman's plays. Four days later came Shumlin's response: he didn't understand the play at all. Baffled by Shumlin's confusion, Miller's old insecurities about his value as a playwright were revived. The play was also sent to Leland Hayward, who was Miller's agent at the time. After a week, Hayward hadn't even picked up the script. Frustrated, the writer went to Hayward's office, demanded the return of all his scripts, and announced that he would be leaving the agency. Realizing the consequences of losing him, the agency secretary asked that *All My Sons* be left with Kay Brown, another agent in the office. Miller agreed, and the next day he received an overwhelmingly enthusiastic phone call from Brown, who called to say she thought the play was terrific. She remained Arthur Miller's agent for the next forty years.

Kay Brown immediately sent the play to Elia Kazan and Harold Clurman, who headed the Group Theater in New York. The two men were already established as major forces in the American theater, both as directors and as artistic producers. The play had also gone to the Theater Guild, the company that originally produced many of Eugene O'Neill's works. Both

Elia Kazan (*right*), a well-respected director, was chosen to direct *All My Sons* for the Group Theater.

companies wanted *All My Sons*, and it was up to Miller to choose between them, an awesome task considering the wonderful reputations of both theaters. It was decided that the Group Theater would do the play and that Kazan would direct rather than Clurman. The playwright particularly respected Kazan's endless energy and constant enthusiasm for new directions in the theater. In the coming years, many other great playwrights, including Tennessee Williams, would share Miller's feelings about Kazan's talent. Kazan

Drama critic Brooks Atkinson praised and defended *All My Sons*.

would bring his unique vision and genius to many
landmark productions, including the original staging
of Williams' *A Streetcar Named Desire* and Miller's
*Death of a Salesman*.

The rehearsals for *All My Sons* went well, and it
became obvious that Miller and Kazan shared a certain
artistic sense about the material that made them opti-
mistic about the project. Working with Kazan, the
playwright was able to rewrite and revise the play

until it contained only what he deemed the essentials. Kazan liked to cut to the core of a play and had little patience for "adornments." "I believed in a kind of biological playwriting," Miller recalls about that time: "nature abhors the superfluous, and whatever does not actively contribute to the life of an organism is sloughed off." By the time the play was in its final draft, it was a compact and powerful work, one that attempted to cut directly to the emotions of its audience.

The play opened in New Haven, Connecticut, in 1947 and was fairly well received. It was obvious to many involved with the production that the play had great impact. By the time *All My Sons* reached New York and Boston, it was, in the author's words, "like a bullet on a straight clean trajectory that rammed the audience back into its seats." The production did quite well in New York (opening in January at the Coronet Theater), despite the fact that its tragic message and moral meaning baffled many critics. Nonetheless, the play established Miller as an important writer and launched him into a new world of fame. The arrival and success of *All My Sons* in 1947 coincided with the birth of Miller's son, Robert, who was born on May 31 of that same year.

Much of Miller's newfound recognition as a premiere American playwright came from Brooks Atkinson, a popular drama critic at the time. Atkinson was one of the few critics who saw the power of *All My Sons* and defended it in the press. He was a strong supporter of theater that was socially vital as well as entertaining. It was due to his recommendations that the play ran for so many months. Atkinson also seemed to be tuned into the theatergoing public at the time, for audience attendance and reaction were impressive throughout the run.

A scene from *All My Sons*. The play was a scathing indictment of how the desire for success may twist one's moral values.

The playwright, too, had an understanding of the mood of audiences in 1947. In *Timebends*, Miller recalls:

> It was an audience impatient with long speeches, ignorant of any literary allusions whatever, as merciless to losers as the prizefight crowd and as craven to winners, an audience that heard the word *culture* and reached for its hat. Of course, there were people of great sensibility among them, but a play had to be fundamental enough to grab anybody, regardless.

Miller goes on to explain that he structured his plays for that impatient audience, always keeping in mind the limits of the people watching. He emphasized action on stage rather than dialogue, and kept the speeches short to hold an audience's attention. Looking back on those days, Miller is thankful that he had to work within such strict guidelines, aware of the fact that they forced him to use economy of language and clarity of action.

The spring after its opening, *All My Sons* won a number of critical awards, among them the Drama Critics Circle Award. Thirty years later a Jerusalem production of the play would be the longest running dramatic play in the history of Israel and would capture the souls of the Israeli audiences, aware of the play's parallels to their own war-torn world.

Even before the public honor of the Critics Circle Award, the writer was becoming uncomfortable with the idea of fame. A few weeks after the play's opening, people were recognizing him on the street; the compulsory greeting and politeness made him feel artificial. He also harbored a certain sense of guilt for his success—guilt for feeling "better" than others, and guilt that he would never be the same person again.

In an attempt to ease his discomfort and ensure his "continuity with the past," Miller went to the New

York State Employment Service office and asked for any job available. The following day he was in Long Island City, Queens, standing all day assembling beer box dividers for minimum wage. It did not take long for him to come to the realization that it was just as unnatural to be working in a factory as it was to be dodging well-wishing strangers on the street. Though he left the beer box dividers behind, Miller was never able to walk away from the guilt he felt about his success.

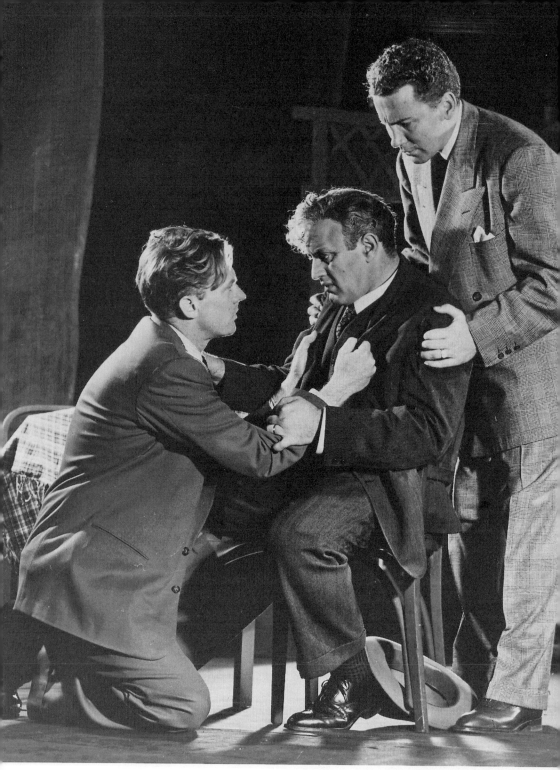

A scene from the original Broadway production of *Death of a Salesman*. Miller's masterpiece explores conflict in the American family and the despair of unrealized dreams.

# CHAPTER 4

# A MASTERWORK COMES TO LIFE

*You know—or do you?—that this play is a watershed.*
*The American theater will never be the same.*
—Lee J. Cobb, to Arthur Miller about *Death of a Salesman*

**B**y 1947 *All My Sons* was firmly established, but the question remained of what project to undertake next. By now, Miller was the father of two small children and had bought a new house at Grace Court in Brooklyn Heights, near the East River. He had resolved not to let success change his style of living; but he couldn't justify remaining crammed into his old apartment with a wife and two small children. Settled into marriage as well as fatherhood, Miller soon decided that a country house—though simple—would also benefit the family. It was around this time that he purchased a small home in Roxbury, Connecticut, a quiet town where he hoped to do some of his writing.

It was during this period—when checks started coming in the mail even when he wasn't working—that Miller realized how the process of royalties actually worked. As a playwright, he was entitled to a percentage of all profits made from any performance or other use of his work. These profits would continue to be paid to him (or his estate) for many years to come—in royalty checks—whenever *All My Sons* was performed anywhere in the world. These royalties offered the writer a new economic freedom and a new outlook on his situation: "I was growing rich and attempting to think poor," he once said. The royalties made him a bit uneasy; he did not entirely like the idea that he could simply walk around the block or read a book and make money doing it. It was just another aspect of his life that would make him feel as if he were losing contact with "ordinary life," the life from which his work had sprung. In some ways, Miller began to feel that his celebrity was causing him to become more distant from his wife and children. Preoccupied with the fear of losing his "artistic self" through fame, the writer felt a need to isolate himself from the world.

As he struggled to maintain his perspective, Miller began to walk endlessly, frequently winding his way over the Brooklyn Bridge and into lower Manhattan. His long walks gave him the time to think about his writing. Soon, without a story or even a concrete idea, a new form began to come to him. It would entail a play the likes of which had never been seen on any stage before, a strange story yet a familiar one. These thoughts were the seeds of *Death of a Salesman*, though other plays would come to life before that work was even started.

New insights about his relation to his work began to emerge on his walks. He realized that he had become fiercely protective of what he wrote. He saw, as his new ideas began to flow, that he was attached to them in an intensely private way. He thought some of his ideas were so personal–so much a part of his "inner self"–that he almost became "ashamed" of his ideas, as though they were, as he described it, some "sexual secret." These feelings of "baring one's soul" through

Miller was constantly struggling to stay in touch with the life of ordinary people. Wandering the streets of New York helped him sort his thoughts and unblock his creative impulses.

writing only intensified the conflict he felt as a playwright who was, by nature, shy. While the writer is not physically out in front of an audience during a play, his *mind* and his *soul* are, through the writing. In many ways this is a much more personal and frightening experience than physically being on stage.

It was during one of these walks over the bridge that Miller first noticed some graffiti that read "Dove Pete Panto?" which means "Where is Pete Panto?" in Italian. He gradually noticed that, near the Brooklyn piers, the same question was written everywhere. This mystery intrigued him, and he decided to do some investigative work. A few days later, he read in a local newspaper that Panto was a longshoreman who had attempted to organize workers against the corrupt union leadership of the International Longshoreman's Association, run by Joseph Ryans and his alleged Mafia colleagues. It seems Panto received a call one night from an unidentified person. He then left the house and was never seen again. The movement to organize longshoremen vanished just as quickly.

By this time, Miller was visiting bars and other local hangouts near the Brooklyn piers asking about Pete Panto. "The idea of a young man defying evil and ending in a cement block at the bottom of the river drew me on," Miller recalled. But the locals would not talk. Miller started showing up on the piers of Red Hook at four in the morning to see what he could learn of this world. It was not long before he realized there were evil forces at work on the piers, though he could not learn more. Soon, he joined forces with two men—Vincent Longhi, a lawyer, and Mitch Berenson, a longshoreman—who had worked with Panto and were willing to show Miller the underground workings of the piers. The writer had gained access to the dangerous world at the water's edge, one that, he said, "drama and literature had never touched."

After becoming part of the longshoreman's world, Miller traveled to Sicily with Longhi to explore the roots of the families from Red Hook. There he contacted many families of the men who worked the Brooklyn piers, conveying messages and passing on information about life in America. He saw a world run by secrecy, by complex organizations of men who operated in a closed society almost identical to the one on the piers. When he returned from Italy, Miller tinkered with a screenplay about the piers but soon scrapped it. He went back to Red Hook looking for a story that was later to become *A View from the Bridge*. But for now, all attempts at starting a Red Hook play fizzled. The ideas and the plot were just not coming. New ideas, however, about another story, were starting to take form.

It was only after his initial adventures on the Red Hook pier that a play about a salesman began crowding out all other thoughts in the writer's head. He had known from the beginning that this play could not be written in a conventionally realistic setting. And he knew enough about the play now to see that the primary force of the main character would come from the fact that, for him, the past was still alive in the present. This idea would involve a "fluid form" that would allow moving back and forth from past to present by verbal transitions. The transitions, he knew, would be punctuated by the music of a lone flute.

For some reason, when Miller decided he was ready to start work on the salesman play, he felt the entire work would have to be completed in one sitting. It was as if he felt a tidal wave of emotion welling up inside him, building up pressure and momentum, a wave that, when it was released, would flow with great speed and force, flooding his pages.

Armed with his notes, the playwright drove up to his country house in Roxbury with the intention of writing his newest play. Upon arrival, however, he was seized with the need for a studio in which to write the play. He also felt the studio needed to be built entirely with his own hands. So, before work on *Death of a Salesman* ever began, Miller's ten-by-twelve studio was first completed.

Miller is uncertain where his love for manual labor comes from, but his affection for carpentry was evident at age fourteen, when he used his savings from a bread delivery job to buy lumber and build a porch for his family's house on Third Street. He borrowed a hammer from his neighbor Manny Newman, a salesman and a man who took manual labor very seriously. The character of Willy Loman is based partially on Newman, who was a small, hardworking person who cared a great deal about what others thought of him. When Manny died, Miller found out that the salesman's only dream was to own a hardware business with his two sons. This sad remembrance of unfulfilled success and love triggered many ideas for Miller while he wrote his play in 1948. Miller remembers Newman:

> That homely, ridiculous little man had after all never ceased to struggle for a certain victory, the only kind open to him in society—selling to achieve his lost self as a man with his name and his sons' names on a business of his own. I suddenly understood him with my very blood.

As Miller built his studio, he would only allow the first two lines of his new play to run through his head: "Willy!" and "It's all right, I came back." When it finally came time to write the play, Miller feared he would never get past those first lines. But when he sat down in his unpainted, sawdust-filled studio that morning in 1948, he launched headlong into the work and wrote the entire first half of the play—the first

The stylized set design and innovative staging helped underscore
*Salesman*'s universal themes.

act—in twenty-four straight hours. When Miller went
to sleep that night, his eyes still burned from weeping
as he wrote and his voice was hoarse from laughing
and shouting out the lines as he heard them spoken by
his characters. He awoke the next day stiff, and
started Act Two, which would take six weeks to finish.

The play Miller created is not simply the story of a
salesman who commits suicide in order to give his
family the money from a life insurance policy. On one
level, the work explores the nature of the American
family, with the father as the power figure, provider,
and example-setter. On another level, the play shows

the toll that business takes on a person in America and the lack of gratitude given to people who devote their entire lives to service in a company.  On still another level, *Death of a Salesman* questions the value of success, which we base our lives on in this country. Throughout the writing, Miller was fascinated by the new ideas he was incorporating.  He was obsessed with "opening up a man's head" for a play to take place within it. He wanted the story to move from past to present with a dreamlike and disoriented quality, portraying the past as just a "dimmer present" that is still, at every moment, alive in us.  These elements give *Death of a Salesman* its immense emotional power.

The two titles he considered most seriously before the final one were *Death Comes to the Archbishop* and *Death and the Maiden*.  He knew his title had to contain the word "death," yet had to be elegant and restrained. His final title, with all its original wording, was *Death of a Salesman: Certain Private Conversations in Two Acts and a Requiem*. This title, with its lack of the specific, emphasizes the universal nature of the story and underscores the "everyman" quality of its main character.

When the play was finally complete, Miller sent a copy to Kazan and then waited by the phone for his response. In a few days, the director called and told the author he thought it was "a great play."  Immediately they began to plan casting for a play that would open in the fall or winter.

Initially, the playwright pictured Willy as a "shrimp" of a man, much the way Dustin Hoffman portrayed him in the highly acclaimed 1984 New York production co-starring Kate Reid, John Malkovich, and Stephen Lang.  But in 1948 both writer and director were struck by the talent of a tall, heavyset actor named Lee J. Cobb.  Though he was completely different from what the author had planned, Cobb, in his reading of the play, showed such enthusiasm and understanding of the character that he could not be ignored. Cobb was cast as Willy, with Mildred Dunnock as his wife Linda, Arthur Kennedy as their son Biff, and Cameron Mitchell as their son Happy.

*Salesman* had its first public performance at the Locust Street Theater in Philadelphia. The audience reaction to it, though positive, was quite unexpected. At the final curtain, there was no applause. The emotions the play stirred were so great that many were too overcome to applaud. Some audience members could be seen holding their faces in their hands as the lights came up in the theater, while others were openly weeping.

The New York premiere of the play, on February 10, 1949, at the Morosco Theater, was a testament to Arthur Miller's new status in the theater world. Celebrities and theatrical devotees were in attendance, all somehow confirming that they were in the presence of one of the brightest stars of the American stage. Brooks Atkinson wrote in his review of the opening night performance of *Death of a Salesman*, "Arthur Miller has written a superb drama. From every point of view it is rich and memorable." Everyone was in agreement; the play was a masterful work.

Though Miller had developed a new "form" for his writing, he did not abandon his conviction that drama should have an important social or political message. The story of Willy Loman, an old salesman who has tragically devoted his life to one company in hopes of attaining the success and respect embodied in the "American Dream," is also the story of failed capitalism. The tragedy of Willy is the tragedy of the underpinnings of American society, and his failure points out our failure. When it first opened, one of the critics called the play "a time bomb under American capitalism," but to Miller, that was not criticism. In many ways, it proved to the playwright that he had been successful. He wrote in his autobiography:

> I hoped it was [a time bomb under American Capital-ism]—or at least under the bull—— of capitalism, this pseudo-life that thought to touch the clouds by standing on top of the refrigerator, waving a paid-up mortgage at the moon, victorious at last.

It was the idea that the seemingly pointless life of a common man could be a tragedy that made *Death of a Salesman* such a landmark drama. Critic Richard Watts, Jr. wrote that *"Death of a Salesman* . . . is one of the most important plays ever written in this country; the essential tragedy of the central figure was not his failure in business or his discovery of the arrival of old age, but his surrender to the false ideals of success." Watts' assessment of this work is by no means unique. It is commonly agreed upon by most theater critics and scholars that this play is a masterpiece with great force. In 1949, the play won the Pulitzer Prize for Drama and would later claim the Critics Circle Award, the Tony Award, the Theater Club Award, the "Page One" Award, and many others.

Arthur Miller wrote an article for *The New York Times* in February 1949, just two weeks after the New York opening of *Death of a Salesman*. The title of the article was "Tragedy and the Common Man," and in it Miller revealed many of the ideas that inspired him to write the drama.

The key idea, and the one that illuminates the critical value of the play, is the notion that "the com-mon man is as apt a subject for tragedy in its highest sense as kings [are]." He goes on to write:

> I think the tragic feeling is evoked in us when we are in the presence of a character who is ready to lay down his life, if need be, to secure one thing—his sense of personal dignity.

From Orestes to Hamlet, Medea to Macbeth, the underlying struggle is that of the individual attempting to gain his "rightful" position in his society.

After scores of people questioned him about how he came to write such a great play, Miller became frustrated by not being able to find a clear answer. In fact, there is no one answer. The best explanation Miller could provide was that the creative process is one in which the "artist blindly follows his nose with his hands outstretched" until he can grasp something and give it form. Often, that form is not clear until the work is finished and only then can an assessment be made of its value.

Asked constantly about *Salesman* and his inspirations for it, the writer recalls that he "came to wish [he] had the sense to say I had learned what I could from books and study but . . . I did not know how to do what I had apparently done and . . . the whole thing might as well have been a form of prayer for all I understood about it." His lack of clarity on the subject of his own creativity was surely, for those who crave clear-cut answers about art, frustrating and confusing. But for others, those who could truly connect with the creative process, Miller's answer simply confirmed that genius can be just as arbitrary as failure.

At the age of thirty-four, Miller won the 1949 Pulitzer Prize for Drama for *Death of a Salesman*.

# CHAPTER 5

# POLITICS AND ART

*The real theater ... is always straining at ... a society that always wants
to deny change and the pain it necessarily involves. But it is in this
effort that ... important work is developed.*
—Arthur Miller

**A**fter winning a Pulitzer Prize and the recognition of much of the world by 1950, the playwright, now age thirty-five, took a trip to Hollywood with his artistic collaborator Elia Kazan. Miller, like other writers who had worked with the director, wrote of Kazan that a certain partnership had developed between them, but Miller always had to keep in mind that "it was an illusion, for in making a play or film people come together primarily as elements of a creating organism and not out of love or mutual regard."

The two men went to California to explore the possibility of making a movie about longshoremen. But Miller was never comfortable in Hollywood, nor was he comfortable with the nature of film and the life of a screenwriter. As it turned out, Hollywood wasn't too interested in Arthur Miller either, not because his work was lacking but because of his alleged political associations with the Communist Party.

By the start of the 1950s there was widespread suspicion that the entire country was secretly being taken over by communists. Almost no one was above investigation, and many government officials, businessmen, sports figures, and people in the entertainment business would have their reputations crushed and their lives destroyed by slander before the decade was over. This era in America, known as the "Red Scare," was fueled by Wisconsin Senator Joseph McCarthy, who led congressional investigations into the private lives and politics of hundreds of American citizens.

In 1950 there was a great deal of risk involved for a Hollywood studio to make movies using "communist sympathizers" or "alleged communists." Certain actors, directors, producers, and writers were actually blacklisted from the industry—no studio would work with them. Working with anyone who was "suspicious" meant risking bad publicity or possibly offending the audience. That, in turn, was bound to have a negative effect on box office sales.

Both Miller and Kazan were fairly well known as "leftists" or "liberals"— even communists. The actual degree to which this was true varied at different points in their lives. However, their politics were undeniably liberal. It was due largely to this political stance that they received a rather lukewarm reception in Hollywood when they arrived to explore the possibility of the "longshoreman's movie." Even the story they described—the tale of a young man who goes against an evil mob that controls the unions—had "anti-democratic" overtones that made most studios uncomfortable. In the end, one man—Harry Cohn of Columbia Pictures—made a deal with Miller and Kazan for the film. The deal involved writing and directing "on spec" (meaning they would not be paid up front and would be compensated only after the movie made back its cost of production). Though the project provided no immediate, or even definite, financial gain, both writer and director agreed to do it.

It was at this time in 1950 that Kazan first introduced Miller to a young actress who had caused quite a stir in several movies and at the many nightly parties that were held around Hollywood. Her name was Marilyn Monroe. Miller was very taken with her, and after a few weeks, the actress and the playwright began to see each other frequently. Miller remembers feeling scared that he would become "desperately attached" to her and never return home. It was this fear that caused him to return immediately to the East Coast to try and forget Monroe.

Miller's long absences from his wife and two children, in addition to his need for isolation while writing at home, had already started to take a more serious toll on the Miller family. The playwright, preoccupied with pursuing his ideas as an artist, became less able to find fulfillment in the role of husband and father. His wife, too, was finding it harder and harder to tolerate the lack of a constant companion and father for her children. Miller was now desperately trying to forget the beautiful blonde starlet he had met in Hollywood. But he soon realized that he could not forget her.

After completing the initial draft of the longshoremen screenplay, entitled *The Hook*, Miller received a call from Harry Cohn. The producer told Miller that he had the premise of the play investigated by the FBI, and that they claimed there was no corruption whatsoever on the piers of Brooklyn. Cohn then asked Miller to rewrite the story so that the "bad guys" were communists and the movie would end in the triumph of democracy. Miller flatly refused, pulled out of the project, and halted the creation of the longshoremen's story once again.

Troubled by the growing pressures he was feeling both as a writer and as a husband, and leading more and more of his social life without his wife, Miller became worried and confused. That year he had also worked on an adaptation of *An Enemy of the People*, a play by Henrik Ibsen. It had failed, and this once again left him dejected and unsure of his abilities as a playwright. He tried to regain his momentum by working on a new piece called *An Italian Tragedy*, but after several months he set that aside too, realizing the piece was simply not working. A few years later, however, much of the work he did on *An Italian Tragedy* resurfaced in *A View from the Bridge*, which began as a one-act play. The year, on the whole, left him unfulfilled in all respects. Artistically, he was unable to grasp and complete an idea that kept its appeal. Emotionally, he became more frustrated by his undeniable attachment to Marilyn Monroe and by the fact that he felt himself slowly slipping away from his wife and family.

By 1951, the Red Scare had an even firmer hold on the minds of most Americans. Senator McCarthy began orchestrating Senate hearings—sponsored by the House Un-American Activities Committee (HUAC)—in which American citizens were questioned unrelentingly about their knowledge of, and involvement in, communist activities in the United States. As this hysteria spread, Miller began to feel the need to react through his writing. As he once wrote, he "sought a metaphor" with which he could shed light on the insanity of the proceedings taking place

Senator Joseph McCarthy spearheaded the Senate hearings in
which American citizens were questioned about their private
political beliefs.

not only in Washington, D.C., but all across the land.
It was during this period that he thought about the
famous witch trials in Salem, Massachusetts, in 1692.

Miller remembered studying the witch trials in a
college history class, but he recalled them as concern-
ing a group of people who believed in matters that
people today dismiss.  As he thought about seven-
teenth-century Salem, coincidentally, *The Devil in Massachusetts*, a book by Marion Starkey, fell into his
hands.  Upon reading it, the entire history of the pe-

riod became clear to him, and he became fascinated with its mysterious rituals and concepts of justice.

At first, Miller rejected the idea of a play about Salem. The whole theme and time seemed too far removed from contemporary life—too irrational for his rational mind to portray believably—and he dismissed it as a possible subject for a drama. But as the suspicion and fear about communist invasions increased, Miller's personal feeling of connection to the Salem of 1692 became stronger and stronger. The more he researched and read, the more the two periods betrayed their similarity. A play, he finally decided, would have to be done.

A historical play such as the one Miller envisioned needed to be researched extensively in order to portray the time and the place accurately. In 1952, the playwright took a trip to the Salem courthouse to begin his search for the information that would provide him with the core of his drama. At the courthouse he was given the public records of the 1692 trials and, as he read them by the dim light of the windows in the town building, he was immersed in the hysteria that had spiraled out of control throughout the small Massachusetts town. The parallels between that time and the present (1952), he thought, were too incredible to believe.

With his time and place determined, Miller set about devising his story and key ideas. He perceived the human tendency to transfer one's feelings of guilt onto others, to "project one's own vileness onto others," and saw it as a fascinating aspect of human behavior. He decided that his play would focus on a sexual infidelity by the main character and would reveal the nature of society and its individuals by dramatizing the community overreaction to the "crime." The play tells the story of a group of young women accused of conjuring up the devil. The town's hysteria soon leads to accusations of witchcraft against many innocent women. The wife of John Proctor, a farmer, is among these and in his attempt to clear her name he is subsequently accused of cavorting with Satan. The play ends with Proctor, who is faced with the ethical choice of either publicly admitting he was possessed by the devil (a lie) in order to be set free, or remaining silent—not naming names—and going to his death.

Once the play was completed, Miller handed it over to Jed Harris who, as director, shaped the work

Miller (*left*), set designer Boris Aronson (*middle*), and producer Kermit Bloomgarden in 1955 mulling over one of *The Crucible*'s production problems.

for its world premiere. Miller's assessment of that first production was not very positive. In his judgment, the play lacked energy and vitality and seemed "stiff" and "formal." It appeared to him that Harris treated the play as a "classical drama," one that needed to conform to classical conventions that were, in Miller's words, "an invitation to slumber." Though the original cast (including Arthur Kennedy and Beatrice Straight) were outstanding talents, the author was not pleased with the production. Well into rehearsal, Harris became seriously ill and had to leave the production, placing the responsibility for direction in the playwright's hands. Toward the end of rehearsals, Harris returned and began making great demands on the producer, writer, and cast. Harris was finally fired—a relief to all concerned—and Miller saw the production through its first performances.

The Crucible's first public showing was greeted fairly enthusiastically in Wilmington, Delaware, but that did little to dissuade Miller from feeling he had "something dead on the stage." By the time The Crucible reached New York in 1953, Miller was convinced that Jed Harris's rehearsal tactics had ultimately ruined his play, and opening night at the Martin Beck Theater in January of 1953 did little to change his mind. Reaction from the audience was more than simply negative—people took an active, and sometimes hostile, dislike to it—yet the reviews, on the whole, were not altogether bad. In a desperate attempt to improve the play's freshness, Miller was forced to take some drastic measures after Straight and Kennedy left the cast for Hollywood. The playwright redirected the play (this time with Maureen Stapleton and E. G. Marshall), removing all the conventional sets and playing the entire piece with the actors, all dressed in black under white lights, set against a

*The Crucible* is a story of fanaticism—a metaphor for past and future political witch hunts. Shown here, in the original 1953 Broadway production, is E.G.Marshall (*second from right*), and Arthur Kennedy (*third from right*).

completely black background. Although this redirection helped to extend the run by a few weeks, the audiences grew more sparse and, after about two months, the play closed.

Richard Watts, Jr., wrote in his introduction to the Bantam edition of *The Crucible* that he believed the play's failure at the time was due in large part to the fact that it was *too* topical for its own good. Watts thought audiences were too threatened by the play's implications to appreciate its force and drama. He also asserted that the parallels the writer was trying to draw were so close that they served to distract more than engage the audience. Watts wrote:

> The contemporary parallels did have a way of distorting, certainly not the truth but the dramatic values, because they distracted one's attention by getting in the way of the story, instead of underlining it, and reminding the spectator almost as frequently of the differences in the two eras as of the shocking similarities.

One of the beauties of *The Crucible*, as Watts suggests, is the fact that it actually *improves* with age. Perspective develops with time, enabling an audience to connect with the force of the drama much more effectively. Since the year of its premiere, the popularity of the play has, in fact, grown steadily. Today, it is Arthur Miller's most frequently produced play. And, in fact, just a few years after its New York opening, a new off-Broadway production was mounted by Paul Libin to rave reviews. With a cast of new young actors and an imaginative director, the play was charged with the energy and vitality it previously lacked. The off-Broadway version ran for nearly two years, and the critics were convinced that Miller had significantly revised the script. But it wasn't the words that had changed; it was the time.

# A PICTURE PORTFOLIO

Miller in China in 1983 to see the production of *Death of a Sales-man*. Chinese audiences praised the play, which transcends any differences between the two cultures.

(*Above*)
The set design for *View from the Bridge*. The play was first performed on stage in 1955 and later made into a film.

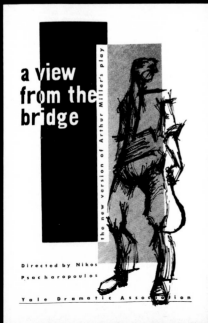

a view from the bridge

the new version of Arthur Miller's play

Directed by Nikos Psacharopoulos

Yale Dramatic Association

(*Left*)
A playbill from a performance of the play at Yale University. Although it did not gain immediate recognition when it was first produced, it has gradually achieved a prominent place in American and international drama.

A scene from *The American Clock*, produced
in 1980. The play, which Miller called a
"mural" of American life during the
Depression, was not well received in the
United States, but was acclaimed in Britain.

Dustin Hoffman (*far right, seated*) played
Willy Loman in the 1984 Broadway and film
versions of *Death of a Salesman*. His performance overcame the critics' skepticism that
only Lee J. Cobb could play Willy.

théâtre royal du PARC

de 26 janvier au 12 février 1967

RENE HAINAUX
FRANÇOISE GIRET

avec

création en belgique

# après
# la
# chute

marcel berteau
léon dony
colette
emmanuelle
marcel josz
nicole lepage
françoise oriane
georges randax
monique verley
denise volny

dispositif scénique de
léonard schach

## ARTHUR MILLER

mise en scène réalisée
par léonard schach

dans le cadre
de la communauté française du théâtre

**Arthur Miller - De dood van een**

Raamteater op 't Zuid

# REALISTICKÉ
# DIVADLO
### ZDEŇKA NEJEDLÉHO

Pondělí

ARTHUR MILLER
# VZPOMÍNKA
# NA DVA
# PONDĚLKY

THE AMERICAN

CLOCK

SPECIAL PREVIEW
of
ARTHUR MILLER'S
NEW PLAY
"THE AMERICAN CLOCK"
at THE HAROLD CLURMAN THEATRE
412 West 42nd Street, New York City
Saturday, May 17th at 8:00 PM
prior to its WORLD PREMIERE at SPOLETO FESTIVAL, U.S.A.

# THE CRUCIBLE

BY ARTHUR MILLER

## MANITOBA THEATRE CENTRE

MARCH 18 APRIL 9 1977

SPONSORED BY LAKEVIEW PROPERTIES LTD. AND METROPOLITAN PROPERTIES CO. LIMITED

The years spent writing and producing *The Crucible* proved to be important ones for Miller's artistic growth. The play, with its pointedly political message, made Arthur Miller a spokesman for the leftist cause, for those people who were being persecuted by the political witch-hunt of the 1950s. It was Miller's voice, striking out in the midst of a national hysteria, that cried disapproval for the direction in which the country was headed. And the power of his message, delivered through his drama, was for the author a perfect example of art that also had a social conscience.

Miller married Marilyn Monroe, the Hollywood film star, in 1956.

# CHAPTER 6

# NEW DIRECTIONS

*One of the strongest urges in the writer's heart, and perhaps most especially the American's, is to reveal what has been hidden and denied, and rend the veil.*
—Arthur Miller

In 1953, a phone call from a friend, actor Martin Ritt, prompted Miller to begin a one-act play for a small theater group in New York City. Excited by the prospect of writing for a troupe of young and eager performers, the playwright completed the play, entitled *A Memory of Two Mondays*, in less than two weeks. Ritt and the actors liked the play but thought they needed another play as a "curtain raiser" to help round out the evening. Free of the commercial worries of Broadway, as well as the grand production requirements of the all-for-profit theater, Miller was inspired to finish his one-act play *An Italian Tragedy*, now known as *A View from the Bridge*. The second play was completed in ten days. It was so good that Ritt laughed upon first reading it, thinking it humorous that the second, much more complex play was intended only as a "curtain raiser."

Unfortunately, the new plays were not destined to be performed by the young troupe. The company lost their theater space and was forced to abandon the idea of producing the new work. With the two new pieces in hand, Miller went to his old friend, producer Kermit Bloomgarden, to propose a possible production. Bloomgarden agreed and in 1955 the two one-act plays had their world debut in New York. Their production prompted Miller to scrap *A Memory of Two Mondays* and to revise *A View from the Bridge* into a full-length drama. The new full-length play, which focused on an Italian longshoreman's struggle to keep his family and his pride together even as he turned over two family members to the department of immigration, was also produced with great success in London by Peter Brook. The play's reception in New York, though respectable, was not what Miller had hoped it would be, and this disappointment only underscored the overall sense of frustration and confusion he now felt in other parts of his life.

By 1955, Miller and Monroe had begun a serious relationship. Though Monroe had divorced her previous husband, Joe DiMaggio, a few months earlier, Miller was still married with children not yet in their teens. In great conflict about his emotions, the writer felt as if his world was "colliding with itself," and a great sense of guilt and helplessness overtook him. And, once again, he was punished for his political beliefs. Having been invited to Brussels, Belgium, for the premiere of *The Crucible* in 1955, Miller was denied a renewal of his passport. Ruth Shipley, chief of the U.S. passport division, explained that it was "not in the national interest" for the playwright to go abroad. This would not be the last time Arthur Miller was punished by the United States for his beliefs.

Soon after the passport incident, Miller began work on a screenplay about juvenile delinquency and gang warfare in America. A young producer had proposed the idea to him and, interested in its social value as well as its dramatic possibilities, Miller accepted the task for very little money. New York City was supposed to help with the production of the film, and cooperation was promised from the police department.

After months of on-the-street research, the writer produced an outline for the story that was heartily approved by all involved, until the American witch-hunt intruded once again. Dolores Scotti, a HUAC investigator, arrived in New York to warn the city officials that having a Communist writing for them could prove to be embarrassing. The city officials were forced to vote on whether or not they would allow Mr. Miller to write their screenplay. Refusing to answer any questions from the committee about his personal beliefs, the author lost the vote by one and was off the project for good.

By 1956, Miller knew that his marriage to Mary was finally over and that he wanted to marry Marilyn Monroe. No concrete explanation has ever been given by Miller for the breakup of his marriage, but his relationship with Monroe and his feelings of alienation from Mary were surely primary factors. To get his divorce as quickly as possible, the writer moved to Pyramid Lake, Nevada, for six weeks to fulfill the residency requirement needed for a speedy Nevada divorce. Living next to him was novelist Saul Bellow (author of *Herzog* and *Humboldt's Gift*), who was in Nevada for the same purpose. Miller found the surroundings calming, quiet, and majestic. "I was trying to make some personal contact with the terrain where I had landed after exploding my life," he once wrote, as he became inspired by the romantic feeling of rootlessness he experienced in the desert.

Marilyn was shooting a movie called *Bus Stop* in Hollywood at that time, and they planned to get married as soon as the film was completed. The actress was gravely troubled by her work on the film and had a difficult time being apart from her fiancé. She dreamed of their life together, living quietly in the country somewhere, simply and without the great pressures of stardom.

Soon after *Bus Stop* was finished (in June of 1956), Arthur and Marilyn were married in a Jewish ceremony at the Westchester home of agent Kay Brown. Marilyn had converted to Judaism in order to marry Miller in a traditional ceremony. Attending the wedding were Brown's husband, Miller's parents Isadore and Augusta, his brother Kermit and his wife, his sister Joan and her husband, the Rostens (Miller family friends), and a rabbi. The ceremony was simple and managed to elude the notice of the media for a few days until word leaked out, and it became front-page news.

Still a newlywed, Miller was subpoenaed by HUAC to testify in Washington about his political affiliations and those of his friends. By 1956, the committee was losing some of its momentum but the writer agreed to "kowtow before the state" even though he realized the absurdity of the gesture. There was never any doubt that he would refuse to disclose names of friends or colleagues that he knew to belong to leftist organizations. Refusals to reveal such information were treated as "contempt of court" charges and were punishable by prison sentences. Miller's refusal brought him a

Miller stuck to his principles during his hearing before HUAC. His two attorneys, Joseph Rauh, Jr. (*left*), and Lloyd Garrison (*right*) managed to keep him from going to jail for not naming names.

contempt charge in 1957 with a jail term, but his lawyer managed to get the sentence overturned on appeal.

The writer's memory of the hearings is imperfect, but he clearly remembers the contempt he had for the entire proceeding and the hypocrisy he saw in being interrogated as a citizen of what was supposed to be the freest nation on earth.

The ultimate irony of that period for Miller was the fact that he was in no way a staunch supporter of the Communist Party—or any other party for that matter.

He was disillusioned by the communists and the way they were organized. "My real view of American Communists," Miller wrote in his autobiography, "was of a sect that might as well be praying somewhere in the Himalayas for all the relevance they had to any motion in the American world."

By the end of the 1950s, the writer's political perspective had changed dramatically, and he had become much less enthusiastic about the ideals of Marxism and communism. This change in Miller's thinking resulted from his observation that deep in the communist doctrine "lies a despairing passivity before History, and indeed power is forbidden to the individual and rightfully belongs only to the collective."

While Miller was appearing before HUAC, a new full-length production of *A View from the Bridge* was being mounted by Peter Brook in London. It received very favorable reviews and played to enthusiastic audiences. The success of the play helped to renew Miller's confidence as a writer and helped to boost his spirits after his frustrating ordeal with the Congressional inquiry into his private life. In many ways, *A View from the Bridge* echoed the writer's earlier themes. This is not surprising given the fact that the basic ideas for the play predated those for *Death of a Salesman*. Along with the shared sense of theme, particularly the tragedy of the "common man" (Eddie Carbone), went a style and tone that evoked the feeling of *All My Sons* and *Salesman*. Otto Reinert writes in his commentary on the play:

> Eddie Carbone's death is only the unavoidable and violent end of a sick man. His suffering is a painful case history, and Eddie himself is pathetic because he is so thoroughly commonplace and likable, "as good a man as he had to be in a life that was hard and even," but he lives and dies in a spiritual darkness that renders his fate ultimately meaningless.

With *A View from the Bridge*, Arthur Miller had once again created a unique tragedy—a tragedy whose scope stems from a small world, yet takes on gigantic dramatic proportions.

Now thoroughly enmeshed in Marilyn's life, Miller became involved in the filming of *The Prince and the Showgirl*, starring Monroe and Laurence Olivier. Again, Marilyn had severe confidence problems during the shooting and was frequently unable to work. Her lack of self-confidence caused Monroe to rely on alcohol and other drugs to function in her roles. Her husband had to spend much of his time and energy attempting to boost her faith enough for her to continue her work. Though he did much to help his wife through those hard times, the filming left him little time and energy to work on anything of his own.

There was, however, one piece he was able to complete for *Esquire* magazine that year, a short story he called "The Misfits." Set in the rugged terrain of Nevada, Miller drew much of his inspiration from his stay there the previous year while waiting for his divorce. The story, which the author said dealt with indifference, loneliness, and isolation, was about "our lives" and about how "meaningless they are and maybe how we got to where we are." Happy with the positive response to his foray into magazine story-writing, Miller was content with "The Misfits" as it was. But soon, as with many events in the artist's life, a unique set of circumstances would prompt him to rework the piece for a much different medium.

Miller on location in Reno, Nevada, 1960, while filming *The Misfits*.

# CHAPTER 7

# "THE MISFITS" BECOMES REAL

*It can take a long time to accept that celebrity is merely a different form of loneliness.*
—Arthur Miller

**W**hile visiting Marilyn, who was in the hospital recovering from an operation for a tubal pregnancy, Miller ran into old friend and photographer, Sam Shaw. During the course of their conversation, Shaw mentioned that he had read "The Misfits" story in *Esquire* and that he thought it would make a terrific movie. He even went so far as to suggest to the author that Marilyn would be the perfect female lead for the film version.

Shaw's suggestions started Miller thinking. The past year had been very tough for them both emotionally—Marilyn in particular—and the failed pregnancy had dealt another crushing blow to Marilyn's self-esteem. Monroe had also become overwhelmed by the pressures of Hollywood and obsessed with the belief that no one took her seriously as an actress. This obsession caused her to become so depressed and paranoid that she was, at times, completely unreachable. As a loving husband, Miller felt a need to do something that would diminish his wife's troubles. He wanted to produce something with the creative power he possessed and give it to her as a gift—a gift that would restore her hope and strength. Miller wrote:

> I hoped that by living through this role she too might arrive at some threshold of faith and confidence, even as I had to wonder if I could hold onto it myself after we had both been let down from expectation such as few people allow themselves in marriage.

Miller finally decided that *The Misfits* could be the gift of faith and confidence that his wife needed, and he immediately began to work on a screenplay.

There were many times during his relationship with Marilyn that Miller had decided he would give up writing so he could lend his wife the kind of emotional support she so desperately needed. So much of their relationship was, for Miller, a tug-of-war between his need to care for Marilyn and a great frustration with having her become an all-consuming preoccupation. She was so needy and looked to him to be her savior. Marilyn's unhappy and unfortunate childhood, as well as the often cruel way in which her beauty had been exploited by people she had trusted in the past, only added to Miller's dream of being the one man in Marilyn's life who would not betray her. But this dream did not often allow for the artist in him to prosper. Often, when the playwright became involved in work, the sharp emotional swings he experienced in his marriage caused him great frustration as a writer. But Marilyn was an inspiration to him as well and, like many famous artists, he found both great energy and paralyzing despair from his emotional life.

Once *The Misfits* screenplay was completed, the writer had to work hard to persuade his wife to take the role of Roslyn. When she finally agreed, Miller contacted John Huston and asked him if he would direct the film. Huston agreed and lined up Montgomery Clift and Clark Gable to play the two male leads in the picture. Gable would portray Gay Langland, an aging cowboy who refuses to confront the realities of a "shrinking frontier" in the American West. Clift would play Perce Howland, a young cowboy with rodeo talent who lacks any direction in his life and who follows Langland out of boredom. The story involves these two men and a beautiful woman (Monroe) as they travel the West in search of a true and rugged existence that makes them feel "alive." In the end, they realize that the "myth" of cowboys and the romance of the West are no longer realities on which they can base their lives.

The screenplay underwent a few revisions before the final shooting script was actually ready and, as soon as the last draft was complete, Huston and his crew moved out to Nevada to set up their first weeks of filming. Making a movie out of his idea was not easy for the playwright. He was uncomfortable with the "artificial" way the camera represented the setting and with the way in which backgrounds were flattened out against extreme close-ups and detail shots. Having had little Hollywood experience, Miller did not know exactly what to expect and, as a result, was constantly disappointed with the results. As a playwright, he was also accustomed to seeing his story progress in sequence, unlike moviemaking, in which scenes are filmed completely out of sequence. The

Along with Marilyn Monroe, *The Misfits* starred Clark Gable (*right*) and Montgomery Clift. All three stars would die shortly after completing the film.

incredible amount of time required between scenes frustrated the writer and left him bored and idle during much of the filming.

But there was more to Miller's frustration with *The Misfits* than the slow process of moviemaking. Marilyn had succumbed once again to depression, and her self-destructive tendencies resurfaced during filming. As her self-confidence lessened, so did her faith in the film and its crew. She became withdrawn and uncommunicative. She arrived on the set later and later each day. The actress began to consume large quantities of sleeping pills in addition to alcohol and other drugs, which made her virtually useless on the set. Not even her own husband could talk to her. As the days went on, Miller became increasingly estranged from his troubled wife as his own depression deepened. In an interview for *Life* magazine, which was published after her death, Marilyn said of her marriage to Miller that it was for her "not a union of two stable adults, but rather a relationship of a confused child-like woman and a man who represented security." This became painfully obvious during the filming of *The Misfits*.

Toward the end of the filming, Marilyn's state of mind had deteriorated almost to the point of no return. Months behind schedule on the shooting, Huston suspended production for ten days and ordered Marilyn to a hospital for treatment of her drug addiction. Ten days later she was back on the set, sober, filled with energy, and ready to work. With that renewed spirit, *The Misfits* finished shooting in an intense burst of productivity and speed.

The emotional ordeal of filming over, Miller felt both great relief and great despair. His relationship with Marilyn never recovered from those months in the desert and, after the film was finished, they separated. It seemed the pressures of the movie caused a further deterioration in Marilyn's mental state. The very project that was supposed to bring them both newfound happiness was the ultimate cause of the failure of their marriage—and that project had been created by Arthur Miller himself.

The film, though it never received sufficient publicity, was quite well received by those who saw it on its first release in 1961. Even Miller, who had been unhappy with what he saw in the dailies at the end of each day, was happier than he thought he would be with the final cut of the movie. At the end of the shooting, Clark Gable told Miller that he had seen a rough cut of the film the night before, and thought it was the best movie he (Gable) had ever made. Four

Monroe and Miller discussing *The Misfits* with director John Huston. The couple was separated soon after work on the film was completed.

days later, while relaxing on a fishing trip, Gable suffered a sudden heart attack and died.

All in all, Miller's brief encounter with Hollywood proved his worst fears to be well founded. He gained little artistic pleasure from the process of filmmaking and felt uncomfortable with the way his work translated to the large screen. In addition, he had spent too much time dealing with the enormous egos of Hollywood actors and directors and had come to feel that Hollywood existed only to feed those egos—and to rake in millions of dollars doing it. He also blamed Hollywood for taking Marilyn away from him. Though he never dismissed their personal problems, he nonetheless placed most of the blame for Marilyn's unhappiness on the callous moguls of the film industry who cared only about exploiting Marilyn Monroe for all she was worth and upon the cruel and unyielding press that had used its infinite power to both elevate her and destroy her.

Miller married Inge Morath in 1962. Unlike Monroe, Morath was independent and self-assured.

# CHAPTER 8

# MUDDLING THROUGH THE SIXTIES

*Most people would rather laugh than cry, rather watch an actor being hit on the head by a pig bladder than by some painful truth.*
—Arthur Miller

The early 1960s were yet another time of great transition for the writer. By January of 1961, Monroe was applying for a Mexican divorce from Miller, and two months later his mother, Augusta, died at the age of eighty. Though things were over with Marilyn, Miller began to enjoy the company of a young Austrian photographer he had met while still in Nevada with *The Misfits*. The woman, Inge Morath, had been traveling the globe with the world-famous photographer Henri Cartier-Bresson, shooting pictures for the photographic agency Magnum.

The photographer and the playwright were instantly attracted to one another. Still recuperating from his previous marriage, Miller admired the cool and purposeful way in which Inge managed her life and career, and he was drawn in by her engaging independence and her obvious talent with a camera. In a relatively short while, the two were spending all their time together and were discussing marriage.

Once his divorce from Marilyn was official in 1962, Miller married for the third time. Soon after the wedding, their daughter Rebecca was born.

For a year or so following his third marriage, Miller would be filled with mixed feelings. He was happy with his new wife and child and with his other children—Bob and Jane—who were doing well in their respective endeavors. But Miller spent almost all of his time at his home in Roxbury, searching for some new inspiration that would start him writing once again. Much of this time he spent alone, while Inge was in Europe on a photo assignment, and each day that went by without new inspiration and creativity brought a growing sense of emptiness for the writer. Part of the problem was the playwright's disillusionment with the direction the theater was taking at the time. Disgusted by the commercialism and lack of redeeming social value in the works of the era, Miller was not moved to create new works for the theater. He remembers in *Timebends*:

> It was hard to understand why, but a strange futility had crept into the very idea of writing a play. I am not sure whether it was the age we were entering or my own evolution, but wherever I looked there seemed to be nothing but theater rather than authentic, invigorating experience. Practically everything—plays, department stores, restaurants, a line of shoes, a car, a hair salon—was being reviewed as though it had become a self-conscious form of art; and as in art, style was the thing, not content. The tradition that a play of any significance had to address human destiny seemed ludi-

crously presumptuous, was going the way of values themselves. In the theater, it was said, we were in the age of the director, with the playwright his assistant, in effect—but didn't this come from the fascination not with what was being said but how? The very existence of the playwright was under challenge now; it was as though he represented the concept of predictability itself, with his preset speeches and plots that ended in some approximation of order.

Even with his disdain for the state of theater at the time, the playwright realized that without his work to keep him going, he felt useless and unhappy. And so he resolved to start working again and soon found some motivation.

By 1963, Miller was dividing his time between Roxbury and a new apartment in the Chelsea Hotel in Manhattan. It was at the Chelsea that he sought some inspiration to write about the crazy time in which he now lived. But his ultimate lack of interest in the "movement" of the sixties left him barren of ideas. The writer felt that the sixties did so much commenting on itself that there was little chance to say something that had not been said before.

Out of this apathetic feeling came a film scenario entitled *The Truth Drug*—an attempt to explain the sixties artistically. The story, more humorous now for its nostalgic value, told of a young researcher who stumbles upon a chemical that can transpose the most aggressive animal into a loving one. The drug falls into some unlikely hands and, when manufactured, causes some complications. In the scenario, the drug, called "Love," causes professional football to collapse as the players refuse to tackle one another. The subway system grinds to a halt as passengers refuse to push their way onto the crowded cars and, most dangerous of all, the Armed Forces begin ingesting Love, causing submarines to surface so men can sunbathe on their decks instead of completing secret missions against the Russians. Realizing the absurdity of the story, Miller abandoned the project before he wrote an ending.

Gratifying inspiration finally came from researching a theme that had intrigued him since the end of World War II. Miller focused on the scientists who were responsible for building the atomic bombs that were eventually dropped on Nagasaki and Hiroshima to end the war in 1945. At the core of this theme was the idea of the scientist who is in conflict over his dedication to science and his sense of guilt for the destruction his knowledge can create. But the play was about more than guilt. Miller also sought to explore the scientist's personal connection to his or her work. He wanted to see how, in the pursuit of something important, a scientist can become so emotionally involved that he or she can be blinded to the facts.

After a great deal of firsthand research, including interviews with J. Robert Oppenheimer, the scientist who headed the development of the first atomic bomb in Los Alamos, New Mexico, in the early 1940s, Miller began to write furiously in his Roxbury studio. What emerged was a long play, written completely in blank verse, about an Oppenheimer-like character preparing to explode an atomic bomb for a test. When he was finally able to step back from the piece, Miller decided it did not work in that form; that it lacked truth and vitality and must be set aside.

The writer now began to search for another form of drama that would support the dynamics he envisioned for his subject. As he worked, another key element emerged in his thinking: the need—stemming from guilt—to deny responsibility for one's actions. Again he began to write, producing page after page of a play that became too long and drawn out to be a normal production.

Still sorting through his ideas for the science play, the writer took a trip to Germany with his wife in 1964. While there, they visited old concentration camps and attended a trial in Frankfurt of Nazi criminals—some of them doctors and scientists—who were charged with atrocities during the war. At the trials, Miller acted as the official commentator for the *New York Herald-Tribune*. Many of the defendants had carried out hideous experiments on human subjects during the war, all in the name of advancing the scope of science. Many of the issues surrounding the trial were surprisingly relevant to the play Miller had been developing before his trip.

Miller returned from Germany with a renewed sense of commitment to his science play. Having witnessed the testimonies of the Nazis in Frankfurt, he was now even more fascinated by the dynamics of guilt and denial. He decided that his new work would address the issue of "how we—nations and individuals—destroy ourselves by denying that this is precisely what we are doing."

While hard at work on his new endeavor, the playwright received a call from an old friend, the producer Robert Whitehead. Whitehead was now in charge of a new theater project that was underway at Lincoln Center. The project involved the creation of a new repertory theater that would feature new and innovative plays from America's most talented writers. Whitehead wanted Miller to write a play that would open the theater as soon as construction was completed. The playwright was delighted by the prospect. In addition, his involvement in the Lincoln Center project would mean a reunion with his old collaborators Elia Kazan and Harold Clurman, with whom he had not worked in many years. But Miller was worried that he would not be able to finish his play in time for the opening. "I was still swimming through a

Rehearsals of *After the Fall*. Greedy bankers and temperamental artists doomed the Repertory Company project.

couple of hundred pages of dialogue with no sight of the farther shore," he wrote, but he continued to work frantically as the final plans for financing were made with the project's board of directors.

In August of 1962, as he neared the end of the play (now titled *After the Fall*), he received the news of Marilyn's death caused by an overdose of sleeping pills. Though they had not spoken in a while, Miller felt a profound sense of loss at Marilyn's death and a deepened anger at the rest of the world for pushing her to that end.

More disappointment came with the news that the Lincoln Center project was off due to unavoidable differences between the artistic collaborators and the bankers who comprised the board. Left stranded with a newly completed play, Miller and Whitehead worked to produce *After the Fall* in a new repertory theater on West Fourth Street in New York City. The makeshift downtown theater was not ideal—the playwright and the producer were called upon to screw in the seats on the afternoon of opening night (when the roof leaked as well)—and the less-than-perfect facility only served to underscore the author's sense of impending doom.

*After the Fall* was not well received. Looking back on that period in his life, Miller realized that, coming so soon after Marilyn's death, *After the Fall* would have to fail. The writer felt that even though he was able to complete the work, his concentration and critical eye were still unavoidably shaken by the recent tragedy. There were many people, too, who noticed an uncanny resemblance to Marilyn in the female lead character, Maggie, although Miller denied basing his character on his late wife. (Maggie, however, dies of an overdose of sleeping pills in the play.) Much of the audience did not grasp the intertwined themes of guilt and

Joseph Wiseman (*left*) and Hal Holbrook (*right*) starred in the
Lincoln Center Repertory Company's 1964 production of *Incident at
Vichy* at New York's Anta Theater.

denial and many remained confused by the play's unusual mixture of characters, abrupt appearances and disappearances, and transformations of time and place. This "montage" approach did not go over well with the critics either, but the play nonetheless held together well enough for Whitehead to ask for another drama from his friend Miller. As an act of solidarity, the playwright wrote *Incident at Vichy*, loosely based on the life of an old friend, a psychoanalyst who was arrested with false papers in Vichy, France, and was saved by a man he never met.

The play has a strange history; it was the first work by Miller to be banned in the Soviet Union (it was suppressed due to a surge of anti-Semitism in the late 1960s), and it was dropped by three interested producers in France for fear that audiences would resent the play's possible implication that the French collaborated with Nazi anti-Semitism. Finally, in the early 1980s, the play was produced in Paris by Pierre Cardin, but it received defensive and bitter reviews that put an early end to its run.

*Incident at Vichy* was written in a fairly short time. The ease with which he wrote during this period made Miller realize that having a group of vital, young theater people who were willing to work on a piece without concerns of profit and reviews was truly an exciting and inspiring prospect. He remembers thinking that, had he had a "high-level rep theater" or an "art theater" to write for earlier in his career, he would have produced many more plays than he actually did.

As the president of PEN, Miller became an articulate and vocal spokesperson for the rights of writers throughout the world. Here he is shown in an animated discussion with novelist Saul Bellow.

# CHAPTER 9

# THE WRITER AS DIPLOMAT

*My whole life has been a struggle between action and passivity, creation and detached observation.*
—Arthur Miller

In 1965, a phone call from a man he had never met changed the direction of Arthur Miller's life. The Millers had come to Paris to attend the Luchino Visconti production of *After the Fall*. The man on the phone was David Carver, then the president of PEN, an international writer's organization of poets, essayists, novelists, playwrights, and other literary figures. Carver had called to try to persuade Miller to become president of the PEN International Congress. But, not having heard of the organization, the playwright needed a little convincing.

At their first meeting, Carver explained that PEN had been founded by a group of popular writers after

World War I.  Among its founders were George Bernard Shaw, G. K. Chesterton, and H. G. Wells, all of whom believed in the power of the written word to change the way people think.  PEN members hoped that with the shared effort of writers all over the world combating censorship and working for freedom of expression, another war could be avoided.  They hoped that by influencing public opinion and exposing repression and censorship, pressure could be brought upon countries where revolutions were smoldering.  The efforts of PEN did not prevent World War II or any of the many subsequent wars, but they did manage to draw the world's attention to many important political issues that would not have received recognition without the organization.

After Carver's history lesson on the origins of PEN, Miller still wondered why they wanted him.  He had no previous connection with the organization and no desire whatsoever to run any large association.  But Carver explained that PEN needed a prominent name at its helm, a writer with stature who also had a political conscience.  Arthur Miller seemed the perfect choice for such a position.  Carver explained that all the administrative duties would still be carried out by his staff, but the imagemaker, the leader, would be the new president.

After a few days of careful consideration, Miller reluctantly agreed to accept the presidency and was on a plane headed for Bled, Yugoslavia, where the first meeting of the International Congress that he would lead would be convened.  Within a week, the playwright went from complete ignorance of PEN to the top of its organization, making speeches and planning itineraries for upcoming conferences in other countries.  He realized, after some time, that much of his initial attraction to the presidency—and to the association—stemmed from his personal experiences with political intimidation and censorship by the House Un-American Activities Committee in the fifties. He vowed to himself even then that if he could fight against such violations of freedom in the future he would.

As he became more involved in the day-to-day workings of the organization, Miller began to aspire to effect what he considered to be some "real progress." He decided that he would make it one of his primary concerns to persuade the Soviets to join the International Congress. He felt that without the Soviets involved in the issues of global politics and repression, all the debates and all the diplomacy between other countries was somehow losing much of its potential effectiveness.

A number of Soviet writers attended the conference in Bled, at first only as observers. Throughout the conference they remained on the sidelines, watching and assessing the value and honesty of the organization's goals. Miller worked hard to be responsive to their needs and to discuss with them the advantages of their joining PEN. On the final night of the conference, Alexei Surkov, appointed leader of the Soviet "delegation," turned to the president of PEN and announced that the Soviets would like to join the organization if some changes could be made in the constitution to accommodate them. Both Miller and Carver were elated at the prospect of finally having the Soviets take part in their fight for artistic freedom throughout the world. It would take more than a year for Miller to get to Moscow, where he met Surkov in 1967 to complete the final arrangements for Soviet membership to PEN. That meeting remains in the writer's mind as one of his greatest personal achievements. He wrote of that accomplishment, "I was proud of myself; on one corner of the world's field of battle a sort of truce was apparently about to be made."

The business of PEN kept the writer occupied for the four years during which he held the office of president. But even with his commitments to the organization, in 1968 he found time to begin work on a new play entitled *The Price*. It was the story of two brothers, one a policeman and the other a surgeon, who meet again, years after an angry breakup. They have come together now to divide the family's possessions after the death of their father. As grown men, they are under the illusion that they can rise above their past differences and coexist in a mature and civilized manner. But soon all their anger comes back, all the old emotions are awakened once again, and the brothers part unreconciled.

Within the context of the play, *The Price* explores the inevitability of repetition when the truth is never faced. Miller said of the piece that it showed two characters "doomed to perpetuate" their illusions because the truth was too painful to face. Again, the playwright focused on a central theme of denial, using its dramatic implications to achieve what he considered to be a tragedy.

The initial production of *The Price*—directed by Ulu Grosbard and starring Arthur Kennedy, Kate Reid, Pat Hingle, and David Burns—was troubled from the start. Grosbard had conflicts with almost everyone involved in the production. One afternoon rehearsal stopped cold when Kennedy, Hingle, and Reid got into an angry argument with the director that threatened to halt the entire production.

When the production reached Philadelphia, Grosbard was asked to leave because of irreconcilable differences, and the playwright was left as acting director. This episode only strengthened Miller's earlier conviction that he wished to remain solely a writer so he could leave such problems in the hands of someone else.

*The Price* had a respectable season in New York and went on to play in theaters throughout Europe with some notable international actors. Not a landmark

The play *The Price*, produced in 1968, showed that people cannot resolve conflicts within themselves or with others unless they face the truth.

Miller, shown here at the 1968 Democratic Convention, when he became more deeply enmeshed in politics.

work, the play was nevertheless a well-crafted, finely structured piece, obviously written by a man who had more than thirty years of experience in the theater. Though the play did not break any new ground for Miller, its success was a testament to the fact that, at age fifty, the playwright had become comfortable with his voice and his style and was very capable of continuing to use it effectively.

Also in 1968, Miller was nominated to be a Connecticut delegate to the Democratic Convention to be held that year in Chicago. Torn between a lack of enthusiasm and a feeling of responsibility to remain socially involved whenever possible, Miller agreed to attend the convention.

Chicago during the convention was nothing short of bedlam. Violent protests by students and other citizens who opposed the war in Vietnam raged outside the walls of the convention center. The daily arrests and police beatings of protesters were shown across the nation on the network news. Inside, the convention floor was no less chaotic. For Miller and his fellow delegates, the entire process seemed a parody of itself—useless, chaotic, and a depressing example of just how far American society had disintegrated by the end of the 1960s. The convention only served to highlight the breakdown in American values that Miller perceived. Yet, by doing that, it inspired him to keep his writing alive.

Miller, always the activist, addresses an anti-war rally in New Haven, Connecticut, 1968.

# CHAPTER 10

# STAYING INVOLVED

*There are images of such defined power and density that without offering concrete information to the writer they are nevertheless sources of his art.*
—Arthur Miller

In the late fall of 1973, Miller received a reprint of a *New York Times* article. Sent by its author, Joan Barthel, it contained parts of a Connecticut state police interrogation of Peter Reilly, an eighteen-year-old New Canaan boy who had confessed to the brutal murder of his mother, Barbara Gibbons. The boy had been tried and convicted, but residents of his town were so convinced of his innocence that they were emptying savings accounts and mortgaging their homes to raise money for a new trial. The letter that accompanied the article was asking for help for Peter Reilly's cause.

It wasn't until he read the police interrogations that Miller was drawn into the case. The whole procedure seemed both a fraud and a travesty of justice. After twenty-four hours without counsel and ten hours of questioning, the dazed and exhausted Reilly was finally reduced to asking his interrogators if they were sure he murdered his mother, and they, in turn, assured him that he did. Confused and tired, Reilly signed a confession that he retracted after a night's rest. But by then it was too late.

The playwright spent the next five years involved in trying to build a case that would exonerate Peter Reilly. Finally, with the help of some private investigators and lawyers, the boy was cleared. But the whole experience left Miller with a sinking feeling that law and justice were rapidly disintegrating in our country and very few people cared enough to do anything about it.

During the struggle to free Reilly, Miller completed a play entitled *The Creation of the World and Other Business* which, like *The Price*, considered the inevitable failings of human nature and how we, as a society, react to them. The play also explored the nature of God and what kind of psychological situation must have given rise to the creation of God in the first place. Using biblical imagery and parallels, Miller also questioned the enforcement of laws and the nature of justice. This play was truly the product of the years the writer spent involved in the New Canaan murder case.

The years 1976 and 1977 were productive ones for the writer, but not altogether successful ones. By 1976, Miller had completed *The American Clock*, a "mural" of American society during the Depression. A rather unconventional series of scenes and moods, the play failed to reach a significant audience in America. The next play, *The Archbishop's Ceiling*, completed in 1977, was a drama derived from the playwright's travels

A scene from *The American Clock*, completed in 1976.

During Miller's visit to China, he met with that nation's best-known playwright, Cao Yu (*right*). Miller had many conversations with writers about the necessity for creative freedom.

through Prague as president of PEN. It, like *American Clock*, was a highly intellectual piece that attempted to tell a story in unconventional, splintered units of dialogue and action, and its fate in the United States was the same.

Both plays, as the author wrote in his autobiography, were "hard-minded attempts to grasp what I felt life in the seventies had all but lost—a unified concept of human beings." Unfortunately, Broadway was not a receptive environment for risk-taking plays of such intellectual depth. Skyrocketing production costs made it impossible for anything that was not a "mega-hit" to survive in the New York theater. These plays, which evoked moods and feelings through symbolic action rather than conventional dialogue, were far too sophisticated for a Broadway that now thrived primarily on "pure entertainment."

Some plays, such as *The Crucible*, take a while to find their rightful place. Frequently, time must pass before they are accepted; other times they must be produced in other countries before they are appreciated. In the case of *The American Clock* and *The Archbishop's Ceiling*, recognition took ten years and would come from England rather than America. By 1986, both plays were packing London theaters and doing exceptionally well.

Ironically Miller found that television, rather than the stage, was able to handle one of his "hard-minded" plays. In 1979 he wrote the television script *Playing for Time*, a tragic story of a woman who survived the death camps of the Holocaust by playing in an all-prisoner musical group. The Nazis used this makeshift orchestra to calm those marching to the gas chambers.

In the early eighties, Miller created two one-act plays that also tried to explore the conventions of theater in a new and interesting way. *An Elegy for a*

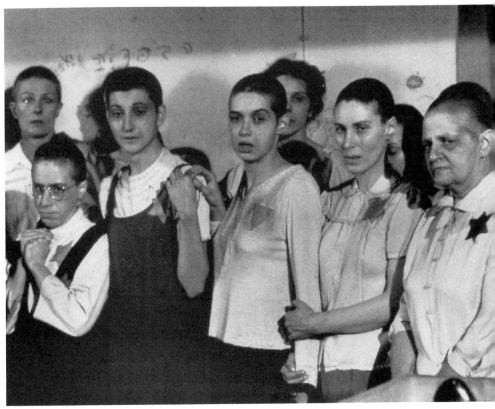

*Playing for Time* is a screenplay written for television. It is about a group of women musicians in a Nazi concentration camp and starred Vanessa Redgrave (*far left*) and Melanie Mayron (*third from right*).

*Lady* was an attempt to write a play with multiple points of view, one for each of the two characters, plus a third—that of the play itself. Miller directed the play in a small space at the Long Wharf Theater in New Haven, Connecticut, in October 1982, together with *Some Kind of Love Story*, the tale of an aging private investigator who is drawn into a case by a woman whose motives are highly suspect. The plays, though awaited with great anticipation, were received with only mild praise. Many critics felt the works were hard to understand, with hidden meanings and vague allusions to seemingly unrelated events.

One of the most rewarding aspects of writing plays—sometimes also the most frustrating—is the

Miller at a rehearsal of *Elegy for a Lady,* which starred Christine Lahti and Charles Cioffi.

fact that they can be constantly redefined: by different actors, by different directors, and for different audiences in different countries. Much of Arthur Miller's fulfillment from the theater in the 1980s has come from his involvement in revivals of his earlier works. In 1983, the playwright traveled to Beijing, China, where the Beijing People's Art Theater mounted a production of *Death of a Salesman.* The fact that this production even existed, much less the fact that it was the first by a foreign playwright in post-Mao China, was unbelievable to most people. What would audiences in Beijing think about a play that was supposed to be so fundamentally American? How could any Chinese citizen understand a salesman and his family? The fact that *Salesman* was an immense success in China only underscored its brilliance and its universality and proved, even to Miller, the play's relevance in other societies.

*Death of a Salesman* was revived on the New York stage in 1984, starring Dustin Hoffman. An artistic as well as a commercial success, this revival illustrated yet another enduring aspect of the play: the fact that Willy Loman could be played as a small, wiry, nervous little man much unlike the burly, exhausted, bearlike Willy as played by Lee J. Cobb. Although there were many skeptics who were convinced that Cobb's version was the only viable one, the 1984 production proved them wrong—much to the pleasure of the proud playwright.

Miller on the set of *I Can't Remember Anything* with star Geraldine Fitzgerald.

# CHAPTER 11

# THE LATER YEARS

*Like every writer, I am asked where my work originates, and if I knew I would go there more often to find more. But there simply are circumstances where plays collect and form, like bacteria in a laboratory dish, later to kill or to cure.*
—Arthur Miller

$\mathbf{A}$s the latter half of the 1980s approached, the playwright became deeply absorbed by the idea of "imploding time," moments when "a buried layer of experience suddenly surges upward to become the new surface of one's attention and flashes news from below." He tried to explore this unique idea in *Danger: Memory!*, two one-act plays written in 1987 for production at the Mitzi E. Newhouse Theater in Lincoln Center. One of the pieces, entitled *Clara*, depicts a man named Kroll, who is shocked when he discovers the body of his murdered daughter. The plot advances as the main character struggles with his fragmented memories that unpredictably begin to surface as he is questioned by a detective. Miller uses certain elements in the piece to illustrate a strange but barely logical connection between the thoughts and memories of the main character. Throughout the play, a slide projector projects giant images that enhance the disjointed nature of the piece. At various points in the play, the dead Clara walks on stage and speaks to Kroll. The companion piece to *Clara*, entitled *I Can't Remember Anything*, was comprised of two elderly characters who also struggle with memory and the unpredictable way recollections can surface and the present can instantly become a forgotten past.

Miller predicted that the New York critics would not connect with the pieces, and he was, of course, correct. But the playwright did receive an unprecedented number of letters from young writers who were very excited by the form and structure of the dramas (particularly *Clara*). "They understood," he wrote, "that I had cast off absolutely every instrumentality of drama except the two essential voices of the interrogating detective and Kroll." Although he didn't find much gratification in the response of the critics, Miller did, nonetheless, find great encouragement from the letters he received regarding *Clara*.

As this book is being written, Miller continues to live quietly in Connecticut with Inge, his wife of more than twenty-seven years. His daughter Rebecca is now a young painter and actress in New York City. Robert Miller, his son by his first wife, is working in the film industry in California, and Jane, his daughter, is a weaver and the wife of a sculptor. The nearly seventy-five-year-old playwright is also a grandfather to Robert's three children.

Miller has lived in his Connecticut home for more than forty years and still "expects to get some play or book finished" in between the time he spends woodworking and caring for his treelined property. But the world is not going by him unnoticed. Each day is most likely critically observed and absorbed into the immense file he has collected on human nature inside his head. And one day, perhaps those new observations will make it to a stage or a screen or a book somewhere where theatergoers can see them and show them the appreciation they deserve.

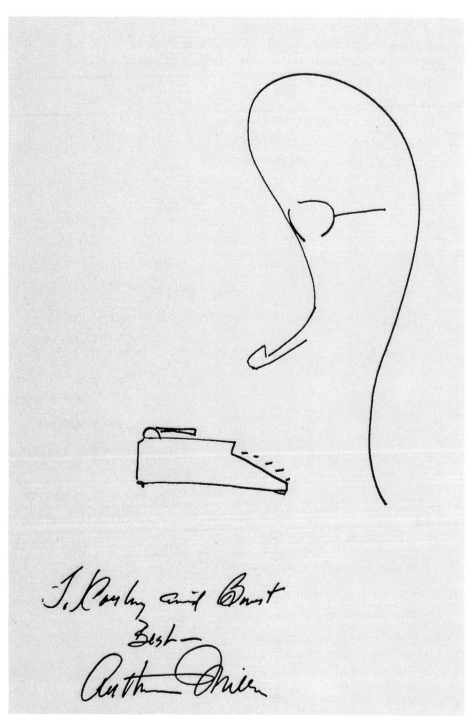

The author's whimsical self-portrait.

# CONCLUSION

*The problem is not that the American Theater has no place for great plays but rather that it doesn't support good ones, the ground from which the extraordinary spring.*
—Arthur Miller

**A**rthur Miller's career as a writer has truly been a collaboration between the life inside his head and the life he actually experienced. Each of his works sprang from a curiosity about the nature of human behavior and a desire to enlighten his audience on issues of social value.

A strong sense of ethics and purpose has stayed with the playwright throughout his life, even when he was in Hollywood and surrounded by the temptations of money and superstardom. But those experiences never shook his dedication to his art and his resolve to keep the integrity of his writing intact.

In tracing Miller's life from its beginning to the present, it is easy to see the relationship between his art and his personal experiences. Circumstance and environment cannot help but play a major role in the development of artists and their work, and, in many cases, these factors can determine whether a writer produces a masterpiece or a flop. For Miller, *The Crucible* would not have emerged if there had been no HUAC or Joe McCarthy; *View from the Bridge* would not have been written if the writer had not stumbled upon the "Dove Pete Panto?" message painted on a wall in Brooklyn; and *The Misfits* might never have become a screenplay if a photographer named Sam Shaw hadn't suggested that it be written. It is evident also, throughout his career, that many people played key roles in inspiring and aiding the creation of the writer's best works. Without them, the name Arthur Miller might never have been known by anyone outside his family.

Much of the playwright's work has, at some time or other, fallen prey to the whims of the American theater. Many of his plays simply appeared "at the wrong place at the wrong time" and failed to take hold because of the political or economic climate of the country. The history of *The Crucible* is a perfect case in point. And perhaps one of Mr. Miller's greatest resentments during his career was the fact that he felt the American theater was unresponsive to serious plays that dealt with "ideas" and attempted to accomplish more than simple entertainment. Much of this unresponsiveness, he felt, stemmed from the fact that professional theater in America was enslaved by the need to make a profit. As Miller sees it, commercialism in the United States has made no place for the works of a serious dramatist. Miller writes:

I have gone through years when my plays were being performed in half a dozen countries but not in New York. Thus, when George Scott did *Salesman* in New York and Tony LoBianco *A View from the Bridge* on Broadway and then Dustin Hoffman *Salesman* again, and a score of other major productions of my plays were mounted in and around the big cities, I seemed to have been "revived" when in fact I had only been invisible in my own land.

Arthur Miller, like any artist in any medium, has had a career that could not have materialized at any other time or in any other place. His work was ultimately part of the world he experienced and many of the twists and turns of his life were simply acts of fate, unpredictable and without a natural logic. For him, the interaction of creativity and experience proved to be successful. For probably hundreds of other writers who came from similar backgrounds, the outcome was uneventful. It is the random nature of experience and creativity that makes the artistic process so interesting and the life of this unique genius so fascinating.

# CHRONOLOGY

**1914** *World War I begins.*

**1915** Arthur Miller is born in Harlem, New York, to Isadore and Augusta Miller.

**1917** *U.S. formally declares war on Germany and enters World War I.*

**1918** *World War I ends.*

**1929** *October crash of the stock market on Wall Street sets off a worldwide economic depression.*

**1933** Graduates from high school and applies for the first time to the University of Michigan, where he is refused admission.

**1934-39** Enters the University of Michigan after convincing the dean that he is worthy. While there, he meets Mary Grace Slattery and wins two Hopwood awards for *No Villain* (1937) and *Honors at Dawn* (1938).

**1940** Marries Mary Grace Slattery on August 5.

**1941** *Japanese attack on Pearl Harbor; U.S. enters World War II.*

**1944** Daughter Jane is born on September 7. Works on *The Story of G.I. Joe* and *Situation Normal* (a book of reportage).

**1945** *World War II ends.*
Publishes *Focus*, his first novel.

**1947** A son, Robert, is born on May 31. *All My Sons* opens on Broadway.

**1949** *Death of a Salesman* opens in Philadelphia and then New York. The play wins the New York Drama Critics Circle Award and the Pulitzer Prize as well as other awards.

**1950** Miller meets Marilyn Monroe in Hollywood. His version of *Enemy of the People* is published.

**1953** *The Crucible* opens on Broadway to mixed reviews.

**1954** *Senator Joseph McCarthy, at the height of his influence, leads televised hearings into alleged communist activity in U.S. army and government.*

**1955** The one-act version of *A View from the Bridge* and *A Memory of Two Mondays* opens in New York.

**1956** Divorces Mary Grace Slattery and, in June, marries Marilyn Monroe. Shortly after the wedding he is subpoenaed by the House Un-American Activities Committee.

**1957** Reworks the short story "The Misfits" into a screenplay for his wife to star in. Congress passes first civil rights bill for blacks since Reconstruction, to protect voting rights.

**1958** *The Misfits* is filmed in Nevada.

**1961** *The Misfits* opens in movie theaters and Marilyn Monroe files for a divorce in Mexico.

**1962** Marries Inge Morath. In August, Marilyn Monroe is found dead from an overdose of sleeping pills.

**1963** *In November, President John F. Kennedy is assasinated in Dallas.*
Begins work on *After the Fall*. In September a daughter, Rebecca, is born.

**1964** *Gulf of Tonkin Resolution is passed, authorizing presidential action in Vietnam.*
*After the Fall* opens to unenthusiastic reviews.

**1965** *President Johnson orders continuous bombing of North Vietnam and pushes the Voting Rights Act through the Congress for passage—a bil'*

*that advanced the rights and liberties of Blacks in America.*
Elected president of PEN and writes *Incident at Vichy*.

1968    *The Price* opens on Broadway. The one millionth copy of *Death of a Salesman* is sold in March.

1969    *Vietnam peace talks begin. Neil Armstrong is the first human to set foot on the moon.*
Retires as president of PEN.

1972    *Watergate story breaks.*
*The Creation of the World and Other Business,* a comedy, opens to lukewarm reviews and closes after only twenty performances.

1973    Miller is appointed adjunct professor in residence at University of Michigan for the academic year 1973-74, and his students work on performing scenes from *The American Clock*.

1974    *President Nixon resigns.*

1976    *The Archbishop's Ceiling* is produced in New Haven, Connecticut.

1979    Completes *Playing for Time*, a screenplay for CBS television.

1982    In October, *Elegy for a Lady* and *Some Kind of Love Story* opens at the Long Wharf Theater in New Haven to mixed reviews.

1983-84    Involved in the production of *Death of a Salesman* in China. In 1984, the play is published in Beijing and revived in New York City in a highly acclaimed production starring Dustin Hoffman and John Malkovich.

1987    *Danger: Memory!* opens at the Mitzi E. Newhouse Theater in New York's Lincoln Center. In April, a Broadway revival of *All My Sons* wins a Tony award. *Timebends*, Miller's autobiography, is published by Harper & Row.

# GLOSSARY

**acclaim** Fame

**anti-Semitism** Anti-Jewish feeling

**aspiring** Hoping

**blacklisting** Outcast, unable to work as punishment for actions or beliefs

**convictions** Strong beliefs

**dailies** Rough film footage that has been shot during one day of moviemaking.

**ethical** Morally correct

**exonerate** To relieve of responsibility or guilt

**hypocrisy** Contradiction

**illuminates** Sheds light on, clarifies

**immigrant** Individual from another country who takes up residence in a new country.

**imploding** Collapsing in on itself

**incarnation** Form, version

**itineraries** Planned schedules

**longshoreman** Worker on the piers

**Marxism** Social theory developed by Karl Marx that advocates the control of the means of a society's production be placed in the hands of the people (the masses) rather than a few individual profit-seekers.

**misconception** False idea

**moguls** Important, usually rich and powerful, individuals

**persecuted** Unjustly hassled

**radical** Advocate of social change through protest and other high-visibility means

**royalty check** Money paid to an author whenever a work is published or performed

**slander** Negative statements or implications that ruin or threaten a reputation

**staunch** Dedicated firmly

**subpoenaed** Officially ordered to appear in court

**superfluous** Unnecessary, needless

**terrain** Landscape, geography

**trajectory** Path, angle of flight

**turgid** Pompous, needlessly overdone

# BIBLIOGRAPHY

Dukore, Bernard F. *Dramatic Theory and Criticism*.
　　New York: Holt, Rinehart & Winston, 1974.
Miller, Arthur. *Timebends*. New York: Harper & Row,
　　1987.
Reinert, Otto, ed. *Drama: An Introductory Anthology*.
　　Boston: Little, Brown and Company, 1961.
Schleuter, June and Flanagan, James K. *Arthur Miller*.
　　New York: Ungar Publishing Co., 1987.
Watson, E. Bradlee, ed. *Contemporary Drama*. New
　　York: Charles Scribner's Sons, 1959.
Watts, Richard. *Introduction to The Crucible*. New
　　York: Bantam Books, 1959.

# SELECTED WORKS

## PLAYS

*All My Sons* (1947)
*Death of a Salesman* (1949)
*An Enemy of the People* (adaptation from Ibsen) (1951)
*The Crucible* (1953)
*A Memory of Two Mondays* (1955)
*A View from the Bridge* (1955)
*After the Fall* (1964)
*Incident at Vichy* (1965)
*The Price* (1968)
*The Creation of the World and Other Business* (1972)
*The Archbishop's Ceiling* (1976)
*The American Clock* (1980)
*Danger: Memory!* (1987)

## OTHER

*Focus* (novel) (1945)
*Situation Normal* (reportage) (1948)
*The Hook* (screenplay) (1951)
*The Misfits* (screenplay) (1958)
*I Don't Need You Anymore* (short stories) (1967)
*Playing for Time* (teleplay) (1979)

# INDEX

## Photo Credits:

**Cover:** UPI/ Bettmann Newsphotos; **Cover Insert:** Inge Morath/ Magnum Photos; **Frontispiece:** Inge Morath/ Magnum Photos; Pages 8, 11, 18: Magnum Photos; 12, 14: The Bettmann Archive; 21, 36, 54, 59: AP/ Wide World Photos; 24, 35, 80, 88, 90, 92, 97, 100, 103, 105, 107, 108, 110: Inge Morath/ Magnum Photos; 27, 30[Barry Hyams], 32, 38[C. Darby, Graphic House], 42[E. Darby, Graphic House], 49, 78: Billy Rose Theater Collection, The New York Public Library at Lincoln Center, Lenox and Tilden Foundations; 45, 61: Dan Weiner/ Courtesy Sandra Weiner; 63: Gjon Mili/ Life Magazine, Time Inc.; 66: Manfred Kreiner/ Black Star; 71: UPI/ Bettmann Newsphotos; 74: Ernst Haas/ Magnum Photos; 82: G. R. Bigelow/ Magnum Photos; 98: Burt Glinn/ Magnum Photos; 114: © 1976 Burt Britton, from the book *Self Portraits* Book People Picture Themselves, Random House, Inc., New York; **Color Insert:** Pages 1, 4A, 5A, 6A: Inge Morath/ Magnum Photos; 2(top): Original set design by Boris Aronson; 2(bottom),8: Billy Rose Theater Collection, The New York Public Library at Lincoln Center, Lenox and Tilden Foundations; 3: Martha Swope.

**Photo Research:** Photosearch Inc.